The Charism of Tongues
A GIFT OF PRAYER AND EDIFICATION

The Charism of Tongues
A GIFT OF PRAYER AND EDIFICATION

Michael J. Sears

Mission West Communications
Santa Maria, California

The Charism of Tongues
A GIFT OF PRAYER AND EDIFICATION

PHONE: 805-937-2766   FAX: 805-937-9114

Library of Congress Catalog Card Number: 96-78109
ISBN 0-9644817-3-1

All Scripture quotes are taken from the New Oxford Annotated Bible, Revised Standard version, Oxford University Press, New York, 1991.

TABLE OF CONTENTS

PART II *(continued)*

The Charism of Tongues in the History of the Church

PART III

The Typology of the Charism of Tongues

DEDICATION

To my beloved mother, Marie Elizabeth,
who loved her children and taught us how to pray.

EXCERPTS FROM POPE JOHN XXIII's PRAYER FOR A NEW PENTECOST

O divine Spirit, sent by the Father in the name of Jesus, give your aid and infallible guidance to your Church and pour out on the Ecumenical Council the fullness of your gifts....

Renew in our own days your miracles as of a second Pentecost; and grant that Holy Church, reunited in one prayer, more fervent than before, around Mary, the mother of Jesus, and under the leadership of Peter, may extend the kingdom of truth, justice, love and peace.

Amen

-Journal of a Soul
Geoffrey Chapman Ltd., 1965

ACKNOWLEDGMENTS

A very special thank you to Rev. Luke Zimmer, SS.CC. for his inspiring spiritual guidance and example as a priest; to Cindy White for her support, prayers and friendship which greatly helped when researching and writing; to Dr. Ronda Chervin and Rev. Mark Avila, O.M.V. for reviewing the manuscript and whose ideas were very helpful; to Rev. Ed Clark for his time, energy and valuable comments in structuring and reviewing the final text; and to Jerrie Castro for her enthusiasm that motivated me to have this work published.

PENTECOST PRAYER OF INTERCESSION

Send Your Spirit

Father of light, from whom every good gift comes,
send your Spirit into our lives
with the power of a mighty wind,
and by the flame of your wisdom,
open the horizons of our minds.
Loosen our tongues to sing your praise
in words beyond the power of speech,
for without your Spirit
man could never raise his voice in words of peace
or announce the truth that Jesus is Lord,
who lives and reigns with you and the Holy Spirit,
one God, for ever and ever.

Amen.

FOREWORD

According to Saint Paul, the only authentic sign of the true Christian is the enduring, lived experience of Faith, Hope and Love. They are the universal gifts of God to every follower of Jesus, His Son. They are the only gifts that endure forever, and the greatest of them is Love. (1 Cor. 13-13).

At the same time, God sends many other virtues and gifts into our lives, gifts for living the Christian life, gifts for building the Christian community, gifts for advancing the reign of God. Among these gifts are the charisms, and among the charisms, the gift of tongues continues to command the greatest attention while remaining the focus of the greatest controversy.

In this work, Father Michael Sears moves the reader beyond the real of controversy and focuses attention on the charism of tongues as a gift that both inspires personal prayer and truly builds up (edifies) the people of God — a gift of prayer and edification.

As Saint Paul proclaims, the gift of tongues is not the sign of a true Christian; it is one charism among many. Nonetheless, it is a most desirable gift. For those who have been given this unique charism, this book will help them cultivate it with better understanding, treasure it with greater love, and use it with greater care. For those whose charisms lie elsewhere, this book will help them understand the true nature of all charisms and find and treasure the ones they have received.

Love alone allows us to understand, treasure, and cultivate the charisms we have received. In the end, however, all other gifts will fade away and only three will remain — Faith, Hope and Love — and the greatest of these is Love.

Rev. Edward W. Clark, S.T.D., S.T.L.
President-Rector, St. John's Seminary College
Camarillo, CA

INTRODUCTION

The charism of tongues is as old as the Church. It was one of the foremost signs manifested through the apostles and the other "first" Christians who gathered in prayer at the feast of Pentecost (Acts 2:1-4). It was a gift that gave tangible evidence of their reception of the Spirit. This gift is referenced in scripture (Acts 2:4, 10:45-46, 19:6; 1 Cor. 12:10, 30; 13:1, 8; 14:1-40), and has been experienced throughout the history of Christianity.

With the birth of Pentecostal movements, spiritual revivals and the growth of the Charismatic Renewal in the Catholic Church in this century, the charism of tongues is now widespread. However, confusion and controversy still exist about the purpose of tongues, and even whether it is legitimate charism. If tongues is cited in scripture, and has been manifested in the Church with good fruit, why does this gift of the Holy Spirit still remain so controversial?

I will attempt to show in this work that the charism of tongues, is a gift of prayer and of edification. And, I hope to clarify and eliminate much of the confusion associated the gift by explaining its unique characteristics.

Tongues has two effects: to edify (build up) the individual and to build up the members of the Church. As it has done in the past, this powerful charism still continues to bring an openness to the human spirit that allows God's Spirit to be received in a new way. I believe it is fair to say that it is one element in Jesus' promise, "I make all things new" (Rev. 21:5). In this light, we can see that the charism of tongues is certainly a drop of "newness" that will eventually increase into a torrent of grace.

A tree is known by its fruit. This is the one analogy that both Jesus and St. Paul give as a guideline for discerning what is from God and what is not (Matt. 7:17-19, 12:33; Gal. 5:22). The fruit that has been experienced by Christians throughout the history of the Church bears witness to the contribution tongues has given to building up the Church. Unfortunately, this gift has not only been misunderstood but condemned, ignored, and abused. Although Paul commanded "do not to forbid speaking in tongues" (1 Cor. 14:39), some have misclassified the fruit that it has produced, and in some instances almost caused the tree to become fruitless. However, the Holy Spirit keeps the trees that bear holy fruit alive and has nurtured this charism throughout the history of the Church.

What exactly is this gift of tongues that edifies? Morton Kelsey, a university professor and well known author, defines prayer in tongues as, "A spontaneous utterance of uncomprehendable and seemingly random speech sounds."[1]

Kevin and Dorothy Ranaghan describe tongues in this

way: "The other word gifts are formed in the language of the one who speaks, while in this gift the speaker has no knowledge of the language in which he speaks. Form and content both are gifts of the Spirit."[2] The late Leon Joseph Cardinal Suenens, Archbishop of Malines, Belgium and a leading advocate for the Charismatic Renewal, views the gift of tongues as "...non-discursive prayer — a pre-conceptual expression of spontaneous prayer — that is within the reach of everybody and remains always in control. It is a verbal expression independent of any specific linguistic structure. In psychological terms, we could say that it is the voice of the subconscious rising to God; finding a manner of praying which is analogous to other expressions of our subconscious in dreams, laughter, tears, painting or dance."[3]

The charism, in its various forms, is fundamentally seen as a gift of prayer. It is a prayer of the heart or pre-conceptual prayer; the mind is not directly involved. There are two terms to distinguish tongues in prayer: *glossolalia* (this term is a modern word derived from the Greek word *glossa* — meaning tongue, and *lalia* — meaning talk or speech) and *xenolalia* (*xenos* — meaning stranger or foreigner). *Glossolalia* occurs when tongues is expressed as language-like, and according to some, contains individual characteristics of language; in the strict sense, including syllables and diction, having similar patterns or structures, but not *identical* with human linguistics.[4]

Dr. William Samarin, a professor of anthropology and linguistics at the University of Toronto states, "When the full apparatus of linguistic science comes to bear on glossolalia, this turns out to be only a facade of language — although at times a very good one indeed."[5] Xenolalia happens when tongues is being expressed in an actual human language (like Spanish, Russian, or Hebrew, for example), and the language was previously unknown to the person praying or speaking it. "If glossolalia is a sign, then xenolalia is God adding to the impressiveness of the sign."[6]

Prayer in tongues can exist under both forms. Although some theologians believe that all expressions of tongues can be classified as xenolalia, others disagree. These differences of opinion will not be investigated here, however, for the sake of clarity, the terms glossolalia and xenolalia will be used throughout this book to differentiate between the expression of tongues as language-like, unintelligible human speech (glossolalia) and as actual human languages (xenolalia).

The charism of tongues is principally manifested as a form of prayer, but not exclusively. Tongues is also an instrument for prophecy, preaching, and evangelization, which can exist as both glossolalia and xenolalia.

The role of the charism of tongues as prayer and as a gift for edifying the Church is what will be discussed. There are three parts to this study. Part I will provide a description of charismatic grace itself and of "baptism in the Holy Spirit." Part II will give scriptural and historical evidence for the charism of tongues. Part III will discuss the different types of tongues and their personal applications; show how this charism of can be exercised as an instrument in pastoral ministries, and finally, give an explanation on how one can yield to the gift of tongues.

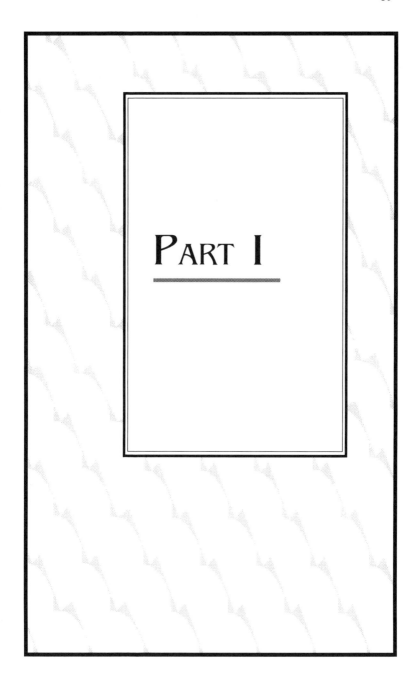

PART I

PART I

CHARISM

Understanding the Meaning of Charism

In order to have a better understanding of the charism of tongues, it is necessary to give a brief description of the etymology or origin of the word charism. The English word comes from the Greek word *charisma* which is derived from the Greek word *charizomai* ("to grant favor," a verb from the word *charis*, "grace") and the suffix -*ma*, which means "work of grace," or "gift of grace." It can also mean "gift of favor," or "gratuitous favor," or a "free gift."[7] The word *ccharisma* is used almost exclusively by St. Paul in the New Testament, except for one reference in 1 Peter 4:10-11. Paul adapted this word from the Greek language and applied it to Christianity to demonstrate the great generosity of God which is bestowed on us through Christ Jesus.

Paul seemed to be describing this when he stated that all comes from God as a gift (1 Cor. 4:7). However, he also used different words for gift (or grace) interchangeably, either to give them the same meaning or to distinguish specific types of grace that operated in different ways.[8] Although he used *charisma* as a general term, even applying it to material gifts, he used it more often as a technical word in reference to spiritual gifts given by the Holy Spirit (1 Cor. 12:7). Paul also viewed charisms as a way of showing differentiation within the Body of Christ, indicating a number of specific roles or functions.

Because God bestows His superabundance of grace in many ways, theologians through history have produced various classifications of grace: sanctifying, actual, sacramental, charismatic, etc. This breakdown does not mean that each grace is separate, but are like rays of light that come from the same source; and when refracted, they produce a rainbow of different colors. So, in essence, there is only one grace, the grace manifested and given to us through the Paschal Mystery of Christ.

To aid in breaking open a deeper understanding of charisms (spiritual gifts), a simple working definition is necessary. Fr. Vincent Walsh gives a concise description: "A charismatic gift is a manifestation of God's power and presence given freely for God's honor and glory and for the service of others."[9]

Charisms in Relation to God's Classical Gifts

Since mid-1960, after the Catholic Church held its twenty first ecumenical council, known as the Second Vatican Council, there has been a deluge of material written about charisms. Although it is not the focus of this book to elaborate on these, it is however, helpful to show the difference between charisms and the other gifts given by the Holy Spirit which lead us on our journey toward God. For instance, what is the difference between the virtues of the Spirit, the seven sanctifying gifts of the Spirit, the fruit of the Spirit, and the charismatic gifts of the Spirit? Are not all these manifestations of God's power and presence, and can they be used to serve others? There are differences between these gifts, but it is also vital to see their interdependence and to understand the movement of the Holy Spirit in the life of individuals as well as the Church as a whole.

First, a virtue is a gift or grace given to form "a habit of good behavior which enables one to do what is right with ease, pleasure and consistency."[10] This grace is given directly to the soul by God as a result of sanctifying grace, independent of the soul, for the soul's own sanctification or holiness (i.e., theological virtues: faith, hope, and love; moral virtues: prudence, fortitude, temperance and justice).

In his book *The Sanctifier*, Luis Martinez, the late Archbishop of Mexico City, comments, "While these principles that the Holy Spirit communicates to the soul in taking possession of it are many and varied, only the theological virtues can touch God intimately. The other virtues purify the soul, remove obstacles to union, draw it nearer to God, adorn it, and beautify it."[11] When these are received the person has the potential to become holy.

Secondly, the "seven sanctifying gifts of the Holy Spirit," wisdom, understanding, knowledge, fortitude, counsel, piety, and fear of the Lord (Isaiah 11:1-3, [LXX] Greek translation) are also effects of sanctifying grace. These gifts, prophesied by Isaiah to be fully present in the Messiah, are now present in Christ, and through Christ are present in all believers who receive the sanctifying grace of Baptism. These gifts work together with the virtues, as Martinez states, "to accomplish the lofty and wonderful operations of the spiritual life."[12]

These seven gifts are like channels in which the virtues are poured into the soul to insure the reception and continuation of the state of being sanctified.[13] The virtues and the seven sanctifying gifts are given for personal holiness and edification. Thus, when people are striving for personal sanctification the Church is also built up. However, these gifts are given for the individual in a *direct* sense and for the community in an *indirect* sense.

The fruit of the Holy Spirit are the result of using God's gifts. They are signs which show that words or actions are from God. Paul lists nine fruit of the Spirit: "But the fruit of the Spirit is love, joy, peace, patience, kindness, goodness, faithfulness, gentleness and chastity; against such there is no law" (Gal. 5:22-23). The presence of only one of these cannot prove the presence of God, but should be discerned in their relation as a cluster or group. Paul does not call them "fruits" of the Spirit but says "fruit," because when a single fruit is present, like peace, one must look to see if the others are present as well. For example, is there love, joy, or even chastity accompanying the fruit of peace?

The fruit of the Holy Spirit is also a gift of consolation.

The fruit that emanates from the gifts of God bring a certain delight or consolation, which allows us to enjoy the virtues, receive the benefits from the sanctifying gifts, and be edified by the charisms.

Even though fruit of the Spirit has the same name as the important virtues, they are not the same. The name is given due to the likeness that exists between the fruit and the virtue. The virtue would be like the tree and the fruit of the Spirit would be comparable to the food which the tree produces. For example, the virtue of love — the divine gift which allows a person to love and be loved by God — produces the fruit of love or the delight of loving, which emanates from the *action* of loving and being loved.

The fruit of the Holy Spirit also reflects maturity and order in the individual who is growing in spiritually. When a tree becomes strong, mature and begins to bear fruit it validates not only what kind of tree it is but, also that it is alive and thriving. Although the fruit does not give life to the tree, it can be the bearer of life to another or transfer life through its seeds. In the same way (unlike the virtues and seven sanctifying gifts), the fruit of the Spirit does not make a person holy or edify like the charismatic gifts. Rather, it validates the presence of the virtues and sanctifying gifts in the soul; confirming the work of the Holy Spirit that perfects and purifies the person. The fruit of the Spirit also validates the presence of charisms within a community as it does in individuals.

Charismatic gifts, as mentioned before, are manifestations of God's power and presence given for God's honor, glory and service to others. They differ from the other gifts in several ways:

1. They are concrete manifestations with characteristics that are experienced in actions such as prophesying, healing, teaching, praying in tongues, acting as an apostle, being faithful to consecrated celibacy, or by living out the specific charism of a religious community. They are not abstract because the Holy Spirit is given with specific, recognizable gifts.[14] The virtues and seven sanctifying gifts are not always perceived in the same tangible ways, or through the external senses; they are not actions, like charisms, but enable one to act in the particular virtue or gift.

2. The virtues and seven sanctifying gifts of the Spirit can directly sanctify a person, whereas charisms are not intended to bring personal holiness in and of themselves. This is why Paul describes love, not as a charism, but as a virtue (Col. 3:14), the "grace of grace," the "gift of gifts," because if you do not have love you are empty (1 Cor. 13).

3. A difference which builds on the second is that charisms are not specifically for the individual. They are given *to* us but are given for the purpose of directly affecting the community. The virtues and seven sanctifying gifts are given to affect the individual directly. This is why a person can have many outstanding charisms but not necessarily be growing in holiness.

4. A significant contrast between charisms that build up others and the virtues and gifts that sanctify, is the latter can be used at will by the person; they function in union with the will. If we want to grow in the virtue of hope, then we need to make a decision to hope. One can only love by deciding to love. People cannot have faith if there is no desire or decision to believe. Once we receive the gift of wisdom, knowledge and piety we need to decide to use these gifts to grow in our relationship with God and others. For the virtues and seven sanctifying gifts to operate and grow in our souls, must have an intention to use them.

Although charismatic grace works, the majority of the time, in union with the will of the individual it is not solely dependent on it. It can operate even when the person's will is not in conformity with the will of God; such as manifesting charisms without love (1 Cor. 13:1-3). Jesus tells us in the gospel about people who have powerful charisms but do not have knowledge and love of God. "On that day many will say to me, 'Lord, Lord, did we not prophesy in your name, and cast out demons in your name, and do many mighty works in your name?' And then I will declare to them, I never knew you; depart from me, you evil doers" (Mt. 7:22-23).

Prophecy, exorcism, and the working of miracles are powerful charismatic gifts. Apparently, the Lord wants to impress upon us the fact that some people may exercise these gifts and at the same time not really love or know God. The Holy Spirit has so great a desire to edify the Church that God will use anybody to be channels, even those who have and will turn away from the will of God.

This does not mean God forces the charism on the person or that the charism will not bear fruit for the others. The charism is operating because the person desires the gift, but they can use it devoid of the virtues and thus will not produce the fruit of personal holiness, even though holy fruit can be produced for others by the action of the Holy Spirit.

A good example would be when someone is preaching and unexpectedly the charism of "word of wisdom" is manifested while speaking. In this case, the person becomes an instrument of the gift. This can occur even when an individual does not pray to the Holy Spirit for a manifestation of this particular charism. However, a predisposition is usually already present in the one who is preaching. Even though a person becomes the channel for the operation of charismatic grace, the charism itself is the direct action of the Holy Spirit. On the other hand, gifts of talent are more integral to one's personality.

There is an interdependence that exists in the authentic supernatural gifts of God. The charisms, the virtues, and the seven sanctifying gifts are infused; their origin is directly from God, not from the person who receives them. They all produce the fruit of the Holy Spirit. The charisms and the seven sanctifying gifts are vital for the Church and the individual member, but these gifts are to be used in the virtues, especially love. If not, they will be as life giving as water poured upon rock; they will not penetrate.

The earlier analogy of the tree can also show us how these gifts of the Holy Spirit are interdependent. A tree to grow and mature needs water, air, sun light, and good soil. The virtues could be comparable to the water, because if there is no water the life force of the tree will cease. In the same way, if the virtues are absent the intimacy with God and the spiritual life of the person will soon die. The light and air could be like the seven sanctifying gifts that are absorbed by the soul to help strengthen and transform the spiritual gifts and apply them to all areas of the one's life. And the charisms can be compared to the nutrients in the soil or even fertilizer which gives the person more power to receive and grow in the other gifts, and build up the different parts of the Church. The evidence of this coordination will be the fruit of the Holy Spirit coming forth and showing that God is present, giving life and consolation to the whole person.

Fr. Edward Clark, S.T.D., professor at St. John's Seminary in Camarillo, California points out that charisms are given not because of personal holiness, individual merit or special favor, but are based on need: "Each member works for the salvation of all…and through the exercise of his or her charism becomes the channel of salvation for others, the conveyor of grace to individual human beings."[15] This is how love is demonstrated, through the gifts of God, especially the charisms. The virtues and seven gifts make the individual holy and charisms make the Church holy. The ideal would be holy individuals making up a holy Church.

To authenticate a true charism there needs to be a sign or fruit that tells us that it is of the Holy Spirit. When a charism is operating there is a manifestation or action of the Spirit of Christ, and with this manifestation there is a result: someone prays for a healing in the name of Jesus and a person is healed. What is the result of the healing? Fr. Robert DeGrandis, S.S.J., comments:

> We see again the role of the gifts of the Spirit moving in us to minister love, peace, and joy to other people. In a certain sense if I have the fruits of the Spirit and I am ministering to another with charismatic gifts, what am I doing to them? I am trying to be a channel of the Holy Spirit that they may experience the fruits of the Spirit in them. Is this not a vehicle for communication of spiritual fruit? I love her. She is racked with anxiety and fears. I ask the Lord to heal her. She gets healed. Her faith increases and she experiences peace and joy. What are these but fruits of the Spirit? Are not the spiritual gifts a way we can share the fruits of the Spirit?[16]

Charisms in the New Testament

The New Testament lists twenty-five charisms, but there are innumerable ways that charisms can be manifested because the Holy Spirit knows by what means the Church needs to be a vehicle of Christ's salvation. The New Testament gives ten lists of charisms (Matt. 7:22; Mk. 16:17-18; Rom. 12:6-8; 1 Cor. 12:8-10, 28-30, 13:1-3, 14:6, 26-33; Eph. 4:11;

1 Pt. 4:10-11). In six of those lists, the charism of tongues is mentioned and five of those lists are Paul's: (Mk. 16:17-18; 1 Cor. 12:8-10; 28-30; 13:1-3; 14:6, 26-33). In the lists of Paul, tongues is last in the order of charisms and his reason for doing this is deliberate. Later we will break down the specific teaching of Paul about the charism of tongues, especially in 1 Cor. 14.

One list of charisms given by Paul in the first letter to the Corinthians is sometimes referred to as the nine classical charisms (1 Cor. 12:8-10). Included are word of wisdom, word of knowledge, faith, gifts of healing, miracles, prophecy, discernment of spirits, tongues and interpretation of tongues. Some call this list the pneumatic charisms (*pneuma* in Greek means spirit) or spiritual gifts, thus differentiating between charisms that do not exhibit obvious manifestations of the Spirit, like those of administration, teaching, and service (1 Cor. 12:28-30). The pneumatic charisms are considered more "free-floating" charisms because they are not specifically associated with a particular office, like that of apostle, pastor, or teacher (Eph. 4:11). Some pneumatic charisms have become institutionalized in the sacraments. Gifts of healing, for example, are dispensed many times when sacraments are received, especially in the sacrament of the sick. These gifts are basic to the life of service within the Church even though some may seem extraordinary.

A charism is a supernatural gift, which means it is not like a natural gift of intelligence or athletic ability. For example, xenolalia, the gift of speaking a foreign language without prior knowledge of it, is different from the talent of being fluent in other languages. All the skill and talent that a person may acquire or receive from book knowledge and learning does not equal a charism. Such natural ability is a talent not a charism. God gives natural grace as well as supernatural. A charism is an ability that is not natural. It is supernatural grace that cooperates with the natural. God gives us this grace that works through our humanness; our nature. In the case of tongues, this supernatural gift of prayer is activated through the natural gift of speech.

Charisms and the Mission of the Holy Spirit

Charisms reflect the action of the Trinity. God is known by His actions, and many gifts from the Trinity are manifested in charisms. The greatest gift from the Father is the Son who, as the God-man, manifested the virtues, the sanctifying gifts, the charismatic gifts and fruit of the Spirit in His ministry. The work of Jesus Christ; His life, death, resurrection and glorification continues in the Church by the gift of the Holy Spirit.

Yves Congar, in his work *Mystery of the Church,* demonstrates that all charisms come from Christ through the Spirit, "who distributes them according to the different functions established by Christ for His Church. The Holy Spirit coordinates these gifts to work together in unity."[17]

This action of the Trinity continues in the Church because there is a need for the Spirit to edify the body of Christ. In other words, the charisms are given as "concrete, tangible, humanly perceptible phenomena,"[18] and just as they were signs of the presence and power of the Holy Spirit in Jesus' earthly ministry, the identical presence and power of the Spirit is still visible today.

NEW TESTAMENT REFERENCES TO CHARISMS

Matthew 7:22	Mark 16:17-18	1 Corinthians 12:8-10
prophecy	exorcism	word of wisdom
exorcism	tongues	word of knowledge
miracles	handling serpents	faith
	immune to poison	healing
	healing	miracles
		prophecy
		discernment of spirits
		tongues
		interpretation of tongues

1Corinthians 12:28-30*	1 Corinthians 13:1-3	1 Corinthians 14:6	1 Corinthians 4:26-33
apostles	tongues	tongues	inspired songs
prophets	prophecy	revelation	teaching
teachers	faith	knowledge	revelation
miracles	voluntary poverty	prophecy	tongues
healers	martyrdom	teaching	interpretation
helpers			
administrators			
tongue speakers			
interpreters of tongues			

Romans 12:6-8	Ephesians 4:11*	1 Peter 4:10
prophecy	apostle	prophecy
service	prophet	service
teaching	evangelist	
exhortation	pastor	
contributing		
leadership		
acts of mercy		

*Charismatic ministries - the persons with whom the charisms are emphasized.

TWENTY-FIVE CHARISMS IN THE NEW TESTAMENT

- Acts of mercy
- Administration (governing)
- Apostleship
- Casting out demons (exorcism)
- Discernment of spirits
- Evangelizing
- Exhortation (preaching)
- Faith
- Handling serpents (power over evil)
- Healing
- Inspired singing (hymn or psalm)
- Interpretation of tongues
- Martyrdom
- Miracles
- Pastoring
- Presiding (leadership)
- Prophecy
- Revelation
- Service/helping (ministry)
- Teaching (catechizing)
- Tongues (praying, singing, and speaking)
- Unaffected by poison
- Voluntary poverty
- Word of knowledge
- Word of wisdom

BAPTISM IN THE HOLY SPIRIT

The charism of tongues is intimately associated with what "charismatic" Christians call the "baptism in the Holy Spirit." This "baptism" refers to an experience that is in addition to, or extends from, the sacrament of Baptism.

Therefore, to understand the association of tongues with baptism in the Spirit we must first understand the relation of baptism in the Spirit to the official sacraments of Baptism and Confirmation.

On the day of Pentecost, Peter stood up with the Eleven and announced the ushering in of the new age. They had just encountered the promise of Jesus, "...you will be baptized with the Holy Spirit..." (Acts 1:5). Peter then quoted the prophet Joel, "And in the last days it shall be, God declares, that I will pour out my Spirit upon all flesh. I will pour out my Spirit; and they shall prophesy" (Joel 3:1; Acts 2:17a, 18b). In his inspired message (charismatic preaching), Peter called thousands to repent, be baptized and receive the gift of the Holy Spirit. And they did. It seemed simple enough: Accept the truth of Christ, get baptized by water and the Spirit, and one's life is changed. One is a Christian.

Today, there seems to be a resurgence of the outpouring of the Spirit, especially through the spiritual works of those in the Charismatic Renewal. However, some confusion has arisen about these outpourings. The classical Pentecostal notion of conversion is termed "baptism in the Holy Spirit," but this does not refer to water Baptism. It refers to the final step of a total conversion to Christ so the person can be saved. In the Pentecostal view the evidence of this baptism is an outward manifestation, namely the charism of tongues. In this perspective of salvation, the charism of tongues validates the person's complete conversion to Jesus, and if the gift of tongues is not manifested then the person is not baptized in the Holy Spirit.

The Charismatic Renewal in the sacramental churches, especially the Roman Catholic Church, readily uses the term "baptism in the Holy Spirit," but it means something very different. This phrase has caused some confusion, especially about the necessity of the sacramental Baptism by water and the sealing of the Spirit in Confirmation.

The Experience of "Baptism in the Spirit"

What happens in baptism in the Spirit that is different from sacramental Baptism and Confirmation? Are they the same experience? What is the relation between sacramental Baptism and the charism of tongues? Francis Sullivan, S.J., on studying the remarkable growth of the Charismatic Renewal in the Catholic Church states, "What these people experienced were the changes that took place in their lives. To attribute those changes to a 'release of the Spirit,' to a 'new outpouring of the Spirit,' or to 'being baptized in the

Spirit' is to offer a theological explanation of the cause of what has happened to them."[19]

When Catholics have had a "Pentecostal" experience they use the term "baptism in the Spirit," but with the realization that it is not contrary to the teaching that the Holy Spirit was already given in the sacraments of Baptism and Confirmation. Catholics are to avoid giving the impression that sacramental Baptism is a "mere water Baptism," as though the only real experience of the Holy Spirit is a "Pentecostal" one.

A report known as *The Malines Document* was published by the leaders of the Catholic Renewal in the early 1970's. It gives an explanation of what happens when a person is baptized in the Spirit:

> Within the Catholic renewal the phrase "Baptism in the Spirit" refers to two senses or movements. First, there is the theological sense. In this sense, every member of the Church has been baptized in the Spirit because each has received sacramental initiation. Second, there is the experiential sense. It refers to the movement or the growth process in virtue of which the Spirit, given during the celebration of initiation, comes to conscious experience....When Roman Catholics use the phrase "Baptism in the Spirit" it usually means the breaking forth into conscious experience of the Spirit who was given during the celebration of initiation.[20]

Sullivan, however, has a different view about the distinction of "theological" and "experiential" senses of receiving baptism in Spirit. He says, "According to this distinction (of *The Malines Document*) people are baptized in the Spirit in the theological sense in sacramental initiation, whereas what happens in the Charismatic Renewal involves only the experiential sense of the term."[21]

Sullivan also believes that people who are baptized in the Spirit receive it in the biblical sense, and that the biblical sense includes both the theological and the experiential senses. There is a real imparting of the Holy Spirit; a *new* outpouring in the theological sense, which allows the person to become aware that the Spirit is working in a new way in his or her life (experiential sense).[22]

An overview of the term "baptism in the Holy Spirit" from the Gospels and the Acts of the Apostles sheds some light on the meaning of this spiritual reality promised by Jesus (in both the theological sense and the experiential sense). In the gospels, baptism in the Holy Spirit is heard in the prophecies of John the Baptist when he speaks about the coming of the messianic judgment (Matt. 3:11; Mk. 1:8; Lk. 3:16; Jn. 1:33). In light of Christian interpretation, this baptism is, above all, the outpouring of the Holy Spirit, which coincides with the predictions of the Old Testament.

The gospels also see Jesus as the one who baptizes in the Holy Spirit. James Dunn believes that Luke, who emphasizes the role of the Spirit more than the other gospel writers, also portrays Jesus as the first to receive the baptism in the Spirit, by his submission to the Baptist and by accepting His suffering of the Cross. Once Jesus had experienced the fullness of the Spirit in his humanity, he then gives the fullness of the Spirit as both God and man.

"In terms of Luke's scheme of salvation-history, all this simply means that the new age and covenant does not begin for the disciples until Pentecost. In the second epoch, only Jesus, the pioneer of our salvation, has entered into that age; he alone has been baptized in the Spirit. It is only with the third epoch that the disciples enter into the new age; only when Jesus has been exalted are they initiated into the new covenant by receiving the Spirit; only when Jesus has completed his ministry as Servant and Lamb of God do they experience his ministry as baptizer in the Spirit.... Where only he participated in the Spirit, now the Spirit comes to all his disciples as his Spirit."[23]

In the Acts of the Apostles, Luke shows that Jesus promises the coming of the Holy Spirit, and he records how this is fulfilled. Peter promises the gift of the Holy Spirit with the reception of Baptism (Acts 2:38, 41). Even though there is no specific mention of the use of water, it may be assumed because of other instances when water is used. But there are two incidents of the baptism in the Spirit, where there is no use of water. At Pentecost the Twelve with the other disciples receive an outpouring of the Holy Spirit (Acts 2:1-4), but no water Baptism, and the household of Cornelius where it takes place prior to the sacrament of Baptism (Acts 10:44-46). The word *baptize* is being used in the figurative sense. The Greek word *baptizo* means to dip, immerse, plunge, sink or drench, and seems to have been used as an expression for giving the Spirit. Luke gives a variety of verbs to describe this, "to pour out," "to send," "to give" the Spirit; and the recipient is seen as "being clothed with," "receiving," "being filled," and having the Spirit "come" or "fall upon" one. So, when Jesus is said to baptize in the Holy Spirit, it is simply a metaphor for saying that he sends the Spirit or that his disciples receive the gift of the Spirit.[24]

To use Sullivan's notion then, if the theological sense of the baptism in the Spirit is a real imparting of the Spirit, then it can be said that the biblical sense includes the theological sense. The same can be said of the experiential sense because, whenever in Acts or in Paul's writings the Holy Spirit is received by people, there is a conscious awareness of the working of the Spirit in their lives.[25]

In the Acts, Luke shows how the continuing presence of the Spirit is manifest among the first Christian community (Acts 2:43-47), and he records the experiences of Peter and the other apostles when outpourings of the Spirit were evident (Acts 8:16; 10:44; 19:6). It is also clear in the writings of Paul, especially in his letter to the Galatians where he reminds them, "Did you experience so many things in vain? — if it is really vain. Does He who supplies the Spirit to you and works miracles among you do so by works of the law or by hearing of faith?" (Gal. 3:5).

The argument from Sullivan, which seems to differ from *The Malines Document*, is that the baptism of the Spirit is a *real* imparting of the Holy Spirit, not merely in the experiential sense, but also in the theological sense. It appears that the position taken in *The Malines Document* alludes to "something alien to the Catholic faith in recognizing any giving or receiving of the Holy Spirit except in and through the sacraments. It seems to suspect as unorthodox the idea that one could receive a new sending of the Spirit (in an answer to prayer) that was not a sacrament."[26]

Sacramental Grace and Charismatic Grace

Sullivan also believes that *The Malines Document* suggests the idea that in the sacramental initiation we receive a "total gift of the Spirit," such that there can be no further question of receiving the Spirit, but only of a coming to a conscious awareness of the Spirit already sacramentally imparted. Sullivan makes three points that show differently.[27]

1. "It is not consistent with Catholic theology to think that in the sacraments of initiation we receive a total gift of the Spirit,' including all graces and charisms that we are going to need, and that over time these push through to our conscious awareness. An example of this is the sacrament of Holy Orders which is traditionally believed to involve a new sending of the Spirit with new gifts."[28]

2. Sullivan says the power of the Spirit cannot be explained as a change in a person's subjective consciousness: "Rather, it seems to me that if I become conscious of the power of the Spirit in me, it is because the Spirit really begins to work in me in a new way; such that I am really changed. Now to say that the Holy Spirit begins to work new effects of grace in

me, theologically involves saying that He is present in me in a new way. And if He is present in me in a new way, this means that there must have been a new 'sending' of the Spirit, because the Spirit is present to us precisely as 'sent' by the Father and the Son."[29]

3. "There does not seem to be anything in Catholic theology that says new sendings of the Spirit cannot take place outside of the reception of a sacrament."[30]

St. Thomas Aquinas seems to concur with this notion of the baptism of the Spirit, because he holds that in our relation to the Divine we can develop a *new relationship* with God. God does not change but is present to us in a new way. The Holy Spirit dwells in us, in such a way as to make us new. This newness takes place initially at the moment we are baptized in water and the Spirit, but St. Thomas raises the question whether there is a sending of the Spirit to a person when the Spirit is already indwelling.[31] He gives examples of invisible sendings which are not examples of sacramental grace but of charismatic grace, and there does not appear to be anything in the context to suggest that a new sending of the Spirit can only be received through the sacraments. "There is an invisible sending also with respect to an advance in virtue or an increase of grace.... Such an invisible sending is especially to be seen in that kind of increase of grace whereby a person moves forward into some new act or some new state of grace: as, for instance, miracles, or prophecy, or out of the burning love of God offers his life as a martyr, or renounces all his possessions, or undertakes some other such arduous thing."[32]

If the language that Aquinas uses, "new act" or "new states of grace," has the same meaning as the biblical language of "sending the Spirit," "pouring out the Spirit" or "baptizing in the Spirit," then, Sullivan concludes it is in line with Catholic traditional theology for baptized and confirmed Christians to ask the Lord to "baptize them in the Holy Spirit." What they are really asking for is a "new sending" of the Holy Spirit to start a new work of grace in their lives.[33]

If the baptism in the Holy Spirit can happen without the reception of a sacrament, what is its relationship to the sacrament of Baptism and Confirmation, which are also new sendings of the Holy Spirit? Christopher Kiesling, O.P. gives a concise overview of this relationship. He says that if someone receives the baptism in the Spirit outside the reception of sacramental Baptism, water Baptism is still foundational and fundamental: "...The fundamental baptism of the Spirit accompanies Baptism with water. This baptism of the Spirit is the inner reality symbolized by the Baptism in water, imitative of Christ's baptism in the Jordan when the presence of the Spirit in Him was manifested. The purpose of Confirmation is to make the baptized members of the Christian community more fully aware of their baptism in the Spirit and its implications in their lives."[34]

These sacraments of initiation are baptisms in the Holy Spirit, but they, Baptism especially, give the fundamental gifts (cleansing from original sin, entry into the body of Christ, indwelling of the Trinity, reception of sanctifying grace, etc.) that no other outpourings of the Spirit can offer. Kiesling also shows that the Spirit can be sent after receiving the fullness of the Spirit in Baptism and Confirmation, but he points to the two sacraments as primary sources for being baptized in the Spirit, whether a person is aware or not, or whether the reception is accompanied by charismatic gifts or not. "The Neo-Pentecostal baptism of the Spirit, then, has its roots in both the sacraments of Baptism and Confirmation. It is less dependent on the latter than the former, however, for Baptism is the primary and essential ecclesial celebration of the gift of the Spirit."[35]

When Christ commissioned his Apostles to baptize in the name of the Father, the Son, and the Holy Spirit, He desired all to receive the indwelling of God; the mandate is one that is fundamental to being a Christian. The Pentecostal experience or baptism in the Spirit could be said, as Simon Tugwell, O.P. believes, to be equated with being Christian. "After all, if it is the basic theological characteristic of Christian behavior that it [an experience of Christ] proceeds from the indwelling of the Holy Spirit, then 'Pentecostal' does simply equal 'Christian.'"[36]

The Rites of Baptism and Confirmation

The prayers from the Catholic rites of Baptism and Confirmation themselves demonstrate the continual sending of the Spirit which will enable the person to live a life of holiness and to edify the Church. Consider the prayer of the blessing of the water before Baptism, "By the power of the Holy Spirit give to this water the grace of your Son, so that in the sacrament of Baptism all those whom you have created in your likeness may be cleansed from sin and rise to a new birth of innocence by water and the Hóly Spirit."[37] And again, "Make this water holy, Lord, so that all who are baptized into Christ's death and resurrection by this water may become more perfectly like your Son."[38]

Even though there are numerous gifts given at the moment of sacramental Baptism, the prayers allude to the continuous sending of graces to the recipient: "He anoints you with chrism of salvation, so that, united with his people you may remain for ever a member of Christ who is Priest, Prophet and King."[39] And again, "By God's gift, through the water and the Holy Spirit, we are reborn to everlasting life. In his goodness, may he continue to pour out his blessing upon all present, who are his sons and daughters."[40]

The Rite of Baptism for children includes a commentary statement after Baptism: "…These children have been reborn in Baptism. In Confirmation they will receive the fullness of the God's Spirit. In holy communion they will share in the banquet of Christ's sacrifice…."[41]

If a person receives the fullness of the Spirit in sacramental Baptism, then why do we need anything else? Because the rite recognizes that these sacraments are necessary to initiate a relationship that can lead to the fullness of what God has to offer to us. Fullness does not mean *exhaustability*. But it does imply a guarantee that the recipient can receive all the gifts the Spirit wishes to give, if the person participates in the life of the Body of Christ and continues to ask and be open to new outpourings of the Spirit.

Other prayers in The Rite of Confirmation reveal this truth also. In the prayer before the reception of Confirmation there are references to the Spirit being given to seal the Baptism and to aid in living out this new life in Christ. "He will pour out the Holy Spirit on these candidates…to strengthen them with gifts and anoint them to be more like Christ, the Son of the God."[42] Again, "The gift of the Holy Spirit which you are to receive will be a spiritual sign and seal to make you more like Christ and more perfect members of his Church….Christ gives varied gifts to his Church, and the Spirit distributes them among the members of Christ's body to build up the holy people of God in unity and love….Be active members of the Church, alive in Jesus Christ. Under the guidance of the Holy Spirit give your lives completely in the service of all, as did Christ, who came not to be served but to serve."[43]

The sacraments of Baptism and Confirmation are baptisms in the Holy Spirit, but through the Church God has institutionalized them to show that they are fundamental to entering into the new life to which Christ calls everyone. When the Church dispenses these sacraments to a person, he or she becomes conformed to Christ and the Church, and becomes like a lightening rod to receive new sendings of the Holy Spirit; in this way the individual lives out this new life in the Spirit according to his or her need and the needs of the Church. These new sendings of the Spirit include the other sacraments, especially Eucharist, and non-sacramental charisms which are given also to call individuals and the Church to a deeper union with the Trinity.

The Spirit knows what gifts we need to live out our Baptism and Confirmation, and the charism of tongues is one that can assist us. Because the gifts are given to help us grow and to build up the Church Paul writes, "The Spirit intercedes for us with sighs too deep for words....And he who searches hearts knows what is the mind of the Spirit, because the Spirit intercedes for the saints according to the will of God" (Rom. 8:26-7).

There is definitely an advantage in receiving Baptism and Confirmation because these sacraments guarantee new outpourings of the Spirit. It is God's will that we develop and become more like Him, and that we advance from glory to glory with the new graces and outpourings of the Spirit of Christ. It is basically a matter of being generous in receiving these "baptisms in the Spirit and recognizing that the Holy Spirit is a dynamic presence within us to form us into the likeness of Jesus Christ in the glory of God the Father.

The Charism of Tongues and Baptism in the Spirit

Understanding Tongues and Baptism in the Spirit

Even though the rite of Confirmation states, "In our day the coming of the Holy Spirit in Confirmation is no longer marked by the gift of tongues,"[44] there is no reason why it cannot be. John Hampsch, C.M.F., a leading theologian involved in the Charismatic Renewal, seems to think our sacramental rites, especially Confirmation, have retained a lack of expectancy in receiving charisms which may not allow a person to be as open to receiving charismatic grace. He points mainly to Peter Lombard, the eleventh century canonist, who limited the effects of the grace conferred in Confirmation, especially the New Testament evidence of the charismatic grace of prophecy and tongues. The texts in Acts that mention water Baptism or baptism in the Spirit give evidence of tongues (Acts 2:4, 10:46, 19:6), and the other times when Baptism is given it is implied that something miraculous was witnessed (Acts 8:9-19, 9:17-18).[45]

Another reason why the rite does not emphasize tongues is that faith is more fundamental to receiving the Spirit. Tongues is not the preeminent sign as it was at Pentecost, but also, as the rite states, we know the Spirit's presence by faith.[46]

Baptism in the Holy Spirit brings many graces, blessings and charisms, but the presence of the charism of tongues with this baptism is unmistakable. Presently, of all the spiritual charisms given, tongues is the most frequently experienced, the most obvious, the most controversial and the most misunderstood. And the question might arise, is it possible to have the baptism in the Spirit without the gift of tongues? According to the teaching of the Church, a person who has received sacramental Baptism *is* baptized in the Spirit. But, as shown earlier, there are new sendings of the Spirit (even in sacraments) and there are signs that confirm the sending of the Spirit. The charism of tongues is one of those signs, and it is one that leaves no doubt regarding what has happened. It is a psychological assurance that you have received the baptism in the Spirit. Dr. Kevin Ranaghan, an author and professor of theology at Duquesne University, who has also been involved in the Catholic Charismatic Renewal, comments: "We do not like to call this an "evidence" of the infilling of the Spirit. For certainly one can be filled by the Spirit without the tangible evidence of tongues. Yet from a powerful and expectant confrontation with the Spirit of the Lord the gift of tongues emerges again and again if not as an evidence certainly as a consequence in the lives of many Christians."[47]

When Bishop Joseph McKinney, (at the time an auxiliary bishop of Grand Rapids, Michigan), was asked whether a person can receive the Spirit without tongues, responded, "Yes, you can. But if you do, the prayer dimension of the baptism in the Spirit is not fully operative."[48] This does not mean that the Holy Spirit is unable to work completely in a person who has not received the charism of tongues, but rather that tongues can be a key to opening many facets of this baptism in the Spirit that can lead to new sendings.

Because tongues is a form of prayer, it is the only charism from the list of classical or pneumatic charisms that can be used for individual edification directly (1 Cor. 14:4). Charisms are given based directly on the need of the community. Even though tongues often does operate in the manner of directly upbuilding the community, tongues as a prayer gift, like any form of personal prayer, can also be incorporated as an instrument to help perfect one's deepest personality.[49] The reason for this is, tongues is a form of prayer that opens a new line of communication with God. The Holy Spirit edifies the individual by allowing the person to utter mysteries in the Spirit (1 Cor. 14:2). Fundamentally, the charism of tongues is a response of praise to God; it is a prayer of the spirit. As *The Malines Document* states: "Those outside the renewal who are attempting to evaluate the charism of tongues will fail if it is not understood in the framework of prayer. It is essentially a prayer gift, enabling many using it to pray at a deeper level. This charism should be understood as a manifestation of the Spirit in a prayer gift."[50]

Praise is the highest form of prayer we can offer to God, and when the human spirit is conditioned to offer praise, God desires to respond to the praise. Praise opens the heart, and when the heart is open, the mind is open, and when the mind is open the whole person will respond and receive the gifts of God. Leon Joseph Cardinal Suenens agrees and shows how this charism brings freedom to the human spirit to praise God in a more profound way:

> If St. Paul treats this gift as the least of all — though he uses it himself
> — might this not be because it is, in a sense, a way that leads to the
> other gifts, a small doorway as it were, which can only be entered by
> stooping: like the door into the Church of the Nativity in Bethlehem?
> Humility and a childlike spirit characterize the kingdom of God....The
> gift of tongues, which has nothing to do with the intellect, makes a
> breach in the "reserve" we assume as system of defense. It helps us
> cross a threshold and, in doing so, attain a new freedom in our
> surrender to God. This surrender hands over body and soul to the
> action of the Holy Spirit. It is only a first step by which we learn how
> to yield to the other gifts, but nonetheless it is precious because it
> gives expression, in its own way, to the inner freedom of the children
> of God.[51]

Tongues is the prayer of the heart, not of the mind. Edward O'Connor, a theologian at Notre Dame University, took almost two and half years to come into tongues. Henry Newman of Germany, also a theologian, took eight months.[52] These men probably wanted to pray from the head, but tongues is more accessible through simplicity and humility, not systematic analysis. It takes humility to yield your voice in this way.

The baptism in the Spirit does provide reception of new gifts, but with the charism of tongues there is a humility that predisposes a person to other charisms in a deeper way, although the Spirit dispenses gifts as he wills (1 Cor. 12:11). The Spirit is generous but does not force a gift on a person. Sometimes the gift of tongues is received in a surprising moment, but the Spirit knows the disposition of the person's spirit to receive the gift. If you do not want the gift you will not receive it. But Paul writes, "Seek earnestly all the spiritual [charismatic] gifts" (1 Cor. 14:1). He would appear to want all to desire these gifts.

The gift of tongues is not the essence of the Charismatic Renewal. The real gift is the Holy Spirit. Tongues needs to be put into proper perspective, but it also has its place and needs to be recognized. The gifts of God are boundless and they are not in competition; reception of one does not cancel out the previous. Each charism received is given in collaboration to build up, to add to.

Hampsch demonstrates how the gifts of the Holy Spirit, especially gifts of prayer, operate so intimately together that when there is openness there is harmony:

> ...Suppose you have a house with 10 rooms and you have not found the key to one of the rooms. You are living in nine rooms of the ten. Then you find the key to the tenth room and fix it up with furniture, and brighten it up and it is a favorite den. You have not added anything on to your house, but you have added something to the utilization of your house. You have that access to another room in the house, and broadened the usefulness of it. Think of the rooms as forms of prayer: Liturgical prayer, private prayer, community prayer, formal prayer, recitatory prayer, mental prayer, meditative and contemplative prayer, and spontaneous prayer. Open this new room to tongues prayer and you have new way of praying. You have not taken anything away, but added. It is a gift, it is positive.[53]

Paul never explicitly says the charism of tongues is the least of the charisms. When tongues does appear in his lists of charisms, tongues is placed last in the hierarchy. In one sense it is the least of the charisms, but in another sense it is one of the greatest. It is the least because it sometimes lacks the power to edify the community as other charisms do. When

I pray in a tongue it edifies myself; it is personal self-improvement. It is one of the greatest in the other sense because it is prayer. When you pray in a tongue you glorify God by directly praising Him. Praise is the highest form of prayer, and prayer tongues is a Spirit-directed form of praise. Tongues can edify in the form of prophecy when joined with interpretation of tongues. This is also true in rare occurrences in preaching.

Tongues as a Common Gift

Prayer in tongues is not miraculous in the strict sense. Even though the gift of xenolalia seems to be miraculous, and prayer tongues can be a catalyst to miracles, this charism is not limited to persons who exhibit particular holiness, but it is rather for common usage. Tongues is not pathological. Dr. William Samarin concluded after a long, extended study, conducted in many countries, that the phenomenon of tongues is neither abnormal nor pathological.[54]

The charism of tongues is involved with the faculty of human language, which is the highest animal faculty. Animals have sophisticated language systems, but not as advanced as human speech. Since God has given this unique faculty to the human race, it is appropriate to use this faculty to worship God. Hampsch asks the question, "Just as Christ has made sacred the elements of matter, including the human body, could he not sacramentalize, sacralize, or spiritualize this privileged faculty of speech, like bread and wine in the Eucharist or water in Baptism? The Lord Jesus in the power of the Holy Spirit has done precisely this in this beautiful charismatic gift of tongues."[55]

There are 5000 existing languages today in the world; 3200 written languages and 1800 unwritten languages and dialects. Cardinal Mezzafonti, who lived from 1774 -1849 in Rome, is considered by some to have been the world's greatest linguist. He could translate 114 languages, 72 dialects, and speak 60 languages fluently.[56] Not even George Schmidt, the head of the United Nations Translation Office, who speaks 35 languages, can compare.[57] All the skill and talent that a person may have acquired from book knowledge and learning does not equal a charism. It is a talent but not a charism, as was explained earlier. A charism can be a natural gift, but one that operates under the influence of grace. In the specific charism of tongues, the speaking of another language is the product of grace. The person did not know the language previously and is suddenly speaking it. It is instant acquisition, not the product of natural learning and study.[58]

Precisely because it involves the faculty of speech which all humanity shares, this gift is open to the experience of all who desire it according to the Spirit.

The baptism in the Spirit and the charism of tongues are integral to each other but not equal. The latter is a product of the former. Just as anyone would rather have the most that a giver has to offer, so too Christians should desire what the Spirit of Christ has to offer. But how is one to find out unless there is knowledge of such charisms. People who are ignorant of charismatic theology and of scripture sometimes react in negative ways towards charisms, especially tongues; they will even think that one who speaks in tongues is "crazy" (1 Cor. 14:22). The following section will deal with the scriptural evidence for the charism of tongues, with special emphasis on Paul's instruction in his first letter to the Corinthians.

ENDNOTES PART I

1 Morton Kelsey, *Tongue Speaking,* p. 1.
2 Kevin and Dorothy Ranaghan, *Catholic Pentecostals Today*, p. 27.
3 Cardinal Leon Joseph Suenens, *A New Pentecost?*, pp. 101, 103.
4 William Samarin, *Tongues of Men and Angels*, pp. 118, 128.
5 Ibid., pp. 127-128
6 Ibid., p. 109.
7 Edward Clark, *The Communal Charism of Education*, p. 103.
8 Ibid. p. 105. Rev. Clark shows how Paul used the word *charisma* in general as meaning the gift of eternal life in Christ (Rom. 5:16 and 6:23).
9 Vincent Walsh, *A Key to the Charismatic Renewal in the Catholic Church*, p. 67.
10 Gerald O'Collins, S.J. and Edward Farrugia, S.J., *A Concise Dictionary of Theology*, p. 261.
11 Luis Martinez, *The Sanctifier*, p. 54.
12 Ibid. p. 54.
13 John Hardon, S.J., *Catholic Catechism*, p. 200.
14 Clark, *The Communal Charism of Education,* p. 198.
15 Ibid., p. 152.
16 Robert DeGrandis, S.S.J., *Spiritual Gifts,* "Understanding Spiritual Gifts," Tape #1.
17 Clark, *The Communal Charism of Education*, p. 147.
18 Ibid., p. 146.
19 Francis Sullivan, S.J., *Charisms and the Charismatic Renewal*, p. 59.
20 Ibid., p. 62.
21 Ibid., p. 63.
22 Ibid., p. 63.
23 James Dunn, *Baptism in the Holy Spirit*, p. 43.
24 Sullivan, *Charisms and the Charismatic Renewal*, p. 65.
25 Ibid., p. 68.
26 Ibid., p. 69.
27 Ibid., pp. 69-70.
28 Ibid., p. 69.
29 Ibid., p. 70.
30 Ibid., p. 70.
31 Thomas Aquinas, *Summa Theologiae,* I, q. 43, a.6.
32 Ibid., I, q. 43, a.6, ad 2 um.
33 Sullivan, *Charisms and the Charismatic Renewal,* p. 72.
34 Christopher Kiesling, O.P, *Confirmation and the Full Life of the Spirit*, p. 116.
35 Ibid., p. 116.
36 Simon Tugwell, O. P., "So Who's A Pentecostal Now?" *New Black Friars*, p. 57 (1976): n. 418.

[37] *The Rites, vol. 1*, "Christian Initiation Of Adults," p. 152, n. 222.
[38] Ibid., p. 153, n. 222.
[39] Ibid., p. 160, n. 228.
[40] Ibid., p. 391, n. 70.
[41] Ibid., p. 390, n. 68.
[42] Ibid., p. 334, n. 589.
[43] Ibid., p. 488, n. 22.
[44] *The Rites*, p. 488, n. 22.
[45] John Hampsch, C.M.F., *The Gift of Tongues*, Tape #2.
[46] *The Rites*, pg. 334, n. 589.
[47] Ranaghan, *Catholic Pentecostals Today*, p. 140.
[48] DeGrandis, *Gifts of the Holy Spirit*, "Understanding Spiritual Gifts," Tape #1.
[49] Malcolm Cornwell, C.P., *The Gift of Tongues Today*, pp. 24-25.
[50] *Theological and Pastoral Orientations on the Catholic Charismatic Renewal*, p. 52.
[51] Suenens, *A New Pentecost?*, p. 103.
[52] DeGrandis, *Gifts of the Spirit, "Understanding Tongues,"* Tape #2.
[53] Hampsch, *The Gift of Tongues,* Tape #1.
[54] Samarin, *The Tongues of Men and Angels,* pp. 34-43.
[55] Hampsch, *The Gift of Tongues,* Tape #1.
[56] Ibid.
[57] Ibid.
[58] Ibid.

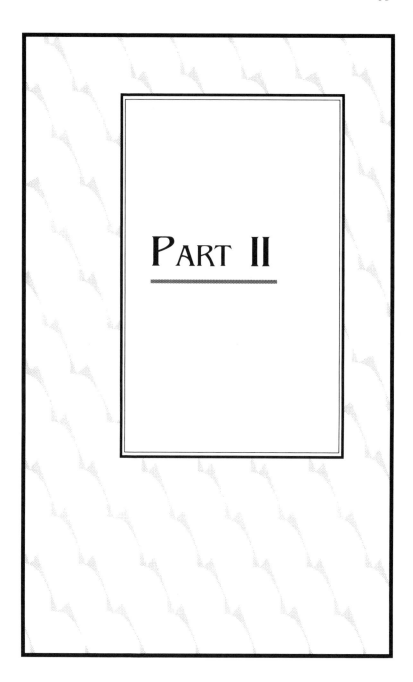

PART II

PART II

THE CHARISM OF TONGUES IN THE NEW TESTAMENT

Tongues in the Gospel of Mark

There are thirty allusions to the charism of tongues in the New Testament. The Gospel of Mark is the only gospel to mention tongues, and does so in its list of signs that will follow believers. "And these signs will accompany those who believe: By using my name they will cast out demons; they will speak in new tongues;...they will lay their hands on the sick, and they will recover..." (Mk. 16:17). Most Bible scholars believe that verses 9-20 of chapter 16 were not part of the original text of Mark. Some of the scholars have the opinion that they were added to bring the gospel to a more distinct closure, while others think it was to show that Jesus promised these gifts and to possibly harmonize this section (which is canonically accepted as inspired) with the Acts of the Apostles.[59]

Tongues in Luke - Acts

The charism of tongues is clearly demonstrated in the Acts of the Apostles. And, since author of Luke is also the author of Acts, we need to have an understanding of the Holy Spirit in the Gospel of Luke if we are going to gain deeper insight in to tongues as referenced in Acts.

As mentioned before, there is no reference to tongues in the Gospel of Luke. Probably this is because Luke-Acts was written as a whole. Another reason is that the undeniable presence of the Spirit, manifested in tongues, had not been poured out (made evident) prior to the Lord's ascension.

The author of Luke-Acts wants to demonstrate that Jesus is the one who brings a new relationship with the Holy Spirit. This action of the Spirit is consistent. The Spirit is present from the beginning in the incarnation of Christ (Lk. 1:35), and at his Baptism in the Jordan by John, when He is anointed with the Spirit and marked as the Anointed One (Lk. 3:22). Unlike the prophets in the Old Testament, wherein the Spirit of God comes upon them only when they are prophesying or working miracles, the Spirit not only comes upon Jesus, but he is "full of the Holy Spirit" permanently (Lk. 4:1). After his resurrection and ascension, the pouring out of the Spirit and the reception of the Spirit by his followers begins with the apostles (Acts. 1-2-2).[60]

In Luke-Acts, the word *glossa* is used as the Old Testament uses it, as a physical member of the mouth, or as a reference to foreign nations and languages, but not as an ecstatic utterance. In seems that Luke wants to differentiate *glossa* from any unconscious speech since many seers or prophets of pagan religions demonstrated the use of "ecstatic" utterances to claim communication from a deity.[61] In the Pentecost experience Luke shows that, even though the apostles demonstrated great joy, they were very conscious of their speech. Also, it is unknown whether the apostles were actually speaking in the known languages (xenolalia) of the people present in Jerusalem, or whether they were speaking in unknown speech (glossolalia) and the people were hearing in their own languages. In any event, the praise of God by the apostles was anointed by the Holy Spirit and the people understood what they were saying.

The Holy Spirit gives this charism to make his presence known in an undeniable way. At Pentecost it not only attracted the people but anointed the hearers by preparing them to receive the proclamation by Peter that Jesus of Nazareth had been raised from the dead. This charism of tongues was seen not only as a sign of the presence of the Spirit of Christ, but also as a new way in which God will manifest Himself. Vincent Walsh comments: "There were many manifestations of God's power and activity in the Old Testament. There were healings, miracles, and people were raised from the dead. These same manifestations were also evident in Christ's life. However, the phenomenon of people praying in tongues is first reported at Pentecost, and was a clear sign of the gift of the Spirit promised by Christ."[62]

James Dunn also comments on Pentecost: "In one sense...Pentecost can never be repeated — for the new age is here and cannot be ushered in again. But in another sense, Pentecost, or rather the experience of Pentecost, can and must be repeated in the experience of all who would become Christians. As the day of Pentecost was once the doorway into the new age, so entry into the new age can only be made through that doorway, that is, through receiving the same Spirit and the same baptism in the Spirit as did the 120."[63] Dunn's text is not referring to "New Age" spirituality, a major trend in this late twentieth century, but about the renewal of spiritual life, and for many a "new actualization" or outpouring of the one true God's Holy Spirit.

The presence of the charism of tongues emerges two additional times in the book of Acts: in the scene preceding the water Baptism of the household of Cornelius by Peter (Acts 10:44-46) and then with the twelve men whom Paul encounters in Ephesus (Acts 19:1-7). The outpouring of the Spirit in both of these passages reflects Pentecost in the faith of the persons involved and by manifestations of the Holy Spirit. These two narratives point to one main notion that Luke seemingly desires to make clear: A person is not Christian without the reception of the Holy Spirit.

When Cornelius and the others encountered the Spirit, Peter was preaching to them about the life, death, and resurrection of Jesus and about the forgiveness of sins through faith. It was at this point that they began to speak in tongues and praise God. In this passage Luke demonstrates two points. First, through the charism of tongues, Christ made his Spirit known to convince Cornelius and the others of the reality of Peter's words and give them a foretaste of Christianity. The manifestation of tongues validated the outpouring of the Spirit which in turn confirmed the truth of Christ.[64] The desire of the household of Cornelius to receive the gift of forgiveness and salvation in Jesus Christ led to the outpouring of the Spirit, and left no doubt about their readiness to receive the gift of salvation and be baptized by Peter. In addition, through the same charism of tongues Peter is made to realize that God is giving the gift of the Holy Spirit to non-Jews as well, and that this can happen in the same way Peter himself received the Spirit at Pentecost. James Dunn concludes, "The meeting with God. ...was divinely effected on both sides, and the divine executor was the Spirit given to those who heard of God's salvation and yearned after it."[65]

In the second instance of tongues being manifested, Paul, who is passing through Ephesus, encounters a group of men who appear to be disciples of Christ (Acts 19:1-7). He wants to make sure that these men are Christian, so he asks them about Baptism and the Spirit. Again, Luke has Paul seek evidence of Christian conversion by a positive response to the question, "Did you receive the Holy Spirit?" The answer they gave was, "We have not so much as heard that there is a Holy spirit." (Acts. 19:2).[66] Therefore, Paul baptizes them in water and lays hands on them for the sealing of the Spirit. It is then that the sign of the Holy Spirit's presence is manifested and witnessed by tongues and prophecy.

Luke clearly conveys the message that the reception of the Holy Spirit is fundamental to becoming a disciple of Christ.[67] And he further proclaims that this baptism in the Spirit is confirmed through signs (charisms); specifically the charism of tongues, which for Luke and his community, is the clearest sign of all.

Praying and Singing in the Spirit

Frequently, the phrases "praying in the Spirit" and "singing in the Spirit," have been designated as terms describing manifestations of the charism of tongues. These aspects of the charism of tongues have been manifested in a variety of ways in private prayer, in group prayer, and in liturgy. Glossolalia and xenolalia, tongues that take the form either of spoken prayer or of singing praise to God, were prominent in the first century Church. "Praying" or "singing" in the Spirit is referenced in several Pauline letters (1 Cor. 14:15; Eph. 5:18-19; Col. 3:16) and in the letter of Jude, verse 20. Does "praying in the Spirit" really refer to tongues? Yes and no. According to Paul's understanding of the Spirit, he knew well that there are other ways to pray in the Spirit, such as, spontaneous singing or praying in the vernacular or the prayer of silence. The mention of psalms and hymns along side of songs in the Spirit in Col. 3:16 and Eph. 5:18 demonstrates this. Just as Paul used the word *charisma* as a general and a specific word for gift, he probably used the terms "praying in the Spirit" and "singing in the Spirit" similarly.

Some bible commentators, however, believe that Paul used these phrases to communicate the inspiring, spontaneous prayer that tongues bring. Most charismatic theologians believe that Paul alludes to tongues as one aspect of the inexpressible groanings uttered by the Holy Spirit in the spirit of a person. From the Letter to the Romans: "In the same way, the Spirit too comes to the aid of our weakness; for we do not know how to pray as we ought, but the Spirit itself intercedes with inexpressible groanings. And the one who searches hearts knows what is the intention of the Spirit, because it intercedes for the holy ones according to God's will" (Rom. 8:26-7).

Scholars in music history support the notion that songs inspired in the spirit have their roots in the glossolalia of the Corinthians and in the "spiritual songs" of the Ephesians and the Colossians. *L'encyclopedie des Musiques Sacres* suggests: "That which concerns the Fathers, just as it had the apostles, was that one sing 'in the spirit' ('with one's heart'). This is the advice of St. Paul repeated to the Corinthians (1 Cor. 14:15) — 'I will sing a song with the spirit' — and to the Ephesians (Eph. 5:18-19) — 'Sing in the Spirit…from your fullness. Recite psalms and hymns among yourselves, and inspired songs; sing and praise the Lord with all your heart.' To the Colossians he said: 'Sing to God with all your heart' (Col. 3:16). St. Jerome recalled this long tradition when he wrote about the jubilus, saying, 'By the term jubilus we understand that which neither in words or syllables nor letters nor speech is it possible to comprehend how much man ought to praise God.'"[68] Jubilus, therefore, is a prayer or song that consists in a rejoicing praise of God. This will be discussed in more detail in the historical section.

The First Letter of Paul to the Corinthians

St. Paul wrote to the Church in Corinth to instruct them in many areas, one of which was the charisms. He wrote to encourage and admonish the Corinthians against errors in their behavior as Christians, but his intention was not to teach everything about the subjects he addressed. For example, he gave a profound and inspired teaching on the Eucharist but did not explain everything about the body and blood of Christ (11:17-34). He gave specific instructions about certain doctrines and activities, but not exhaustively. Therefore, we see that his teaching on the charismatic gifts is no different.

The church in Corinth had a certain affinity for the spiritual gifts, especially the charism of tongues and prophecy. As a result, Paul devotes a whole section of his letter to the faithful of Corinth on how to be balanced in the use of these charisms. Does he encourage the gift of tongues, or does he simply believe that tongues has no use within the assembly? Interestingly enough, Paul supports all uses of tongues, but puts limitations on the use of this particular gift within the community for the sake of maintaining good order in liturgy.

Paul is concerned with preserving unity and with building up of the assembly of people who make up the church. Apparently, the church in Corinth was not only having problems with factions, but also in misinterpreting the basic knowledge that pertained to the foundation of the Christian faith. A number of members were claiming to be "spiritual men" (*pneumatikoi*) because they possessed the "gifts of the spirit" (pneumatika). So, the misunderstandings that arose resulted in a dispute between the prophets and the glossolalists ("tongue speakers"). These short sighted leaders were exalting the charisms of inspiration, namely tongues and prophecy, to the exclusion of other gifts.

Charisms are from the Holy Spirit

In 1 Corinthians 12, the Paul shows how the Spirit of Christ — the Holy Spirit — coordinates everything in harmony. Even a simple utterance of praise to the Lord is given by the Holy Spirit (v. 3). Paul reminds the Corinthians that the charisms are directed by the Holy Spirit, not by the human person.

Paul begins an argument to display a broader understanding of the gifts of the Spirit under the terms of gifts, services (functions), works (vv. 4-6). In order to situate these gifts in a framework that leads to a charitable use, which for Paul is always the up building of the community, he presents an analogy of the body. The teaching of the Mystical Body of Christ is inseparable from the charisms. The body is the community, and just as the human body has gifts, services, and works, so too does the Body of Christ's community. To the claim of the spiritual men that the *charismata pneumatika* (spiritual gifts) are the only gifts, Paul shows a three-fold classification of gifts, services, and works stemming from the same Spirit, thus making them all spiritual gifts. Everything is controlled by the Holy Spirit, especially the charisms of the Spirit.

Paul lists nine charisms that were probably very strong in the Corinthian community:

"To one is given through the Spirit the utterance of wisdom, to another the utterance of knowledge according to the same Spirit, to another faith by the same Spirit, to another gifts of healing by the one Spirit, to another the working of miracles, to another prophecy; to another the ability to distinguish between spirits (discernment), to another various kinds of tongues, to another the interpretation of tongues" (1 Cor. 12:8-10).

Francis Sullivan points out that Paul is explaining that all the gifts come from the same source, the Holy Spirit. "In fact, there is little doubt that in Paul's mind, all these gifts, as 'manifestations of the Spirit,' could rightly be called spiritual gifts, since it is one and the same Spirit who works them all" (I Cor. 12:11).[69] In this context, these charisms encompass that activity whose end is building up of the assembly or the body of Christ and should not be exalted above any other movement of the Spirit. The unity of the Spirit is seen through the charisms when these gifts are put in perspective. This is clear in 1 Cor. 12-14 where Paul teaches about the charisms of the Spirit and how they are to be used in the Christian assembly. Our focus now will be on chapter fourteen.

Tongues and Prophecy

In Paul's beautifully poetic discourse on the virtue of love in 1 Cor. 13, he gives a clear distinction between the call to be virtuous and in being charismatic. Love is the focus and without love even the most profound charismatic experience cannot sanctify anyone. Paul's emphasis is on love, hope, and faith; these will endure even when charismatic grace seems to be absent. The charismatic grace is subordinate to the grace that is distributed in the virtue of love, and Paul reminds the Corinthians of this in order to redirect their attention to the intention of the Spirit — love is primary. What happens then if love is present when these charisms are used? Paul tells us that there be harmony within the church; (1 Cor. 14:12) there will be conversions, and new members will be added to the body of Christ (1 Cor. 14:24).

In chapter fourteen, Paul's argument addresses the factionalism that was present in the Corinthian church. This division was not limited to a single group, but the division between the tongue speakers and the prophets was the most apparent. These two groups were at odds with one another regarding which charism held prominence. Paul clearly shows how the gifts of prophecy and tongues differ; how they are complimentary, and their proper use in the congregation.

Paul criticizes the tongue speakers because they seemed to put undue importance on the gift of tongues. This charism was held to be a clear sign of the manifestation of the Spirit, and among the Corinthians, it may have led to the attainment of greater social prestige in the community.[70] Paul contrasts tongues with prophecy to show that individualism will do harm to the Church, and he tries to point out that these charisms are for the edification of the entire Church in love.

Paul starts chapter fourteen by saying that love should be the prime aim of the Christian (v. 1). It is only through love that the charisms can build up the entire community, as he reminds the Corinthians in chapter thirteen: "If I have the tongues of men or angelic as well but have no love, I am a noisy gong or clashing cymbal" (13:1). On the basis of this, Paul starts the promotion of the spiritual gifts; especially prophecy. By stating that the gifts should be pursued earnestly, he may denote a certain realism in the hint that believers tend to receive the gift they want in faith.[71] But it seems that Paul desires to set the beloved Corinthians straight on the value of the charisms.

Paul immediately defines the function of the gift of tongues, "For the one who speaks in a tongue does not speak to men but to God, for no one can understand him, but he utters mysteries in the Spirit" (v. 2). Paul is indicating the power that the gift of tongues has: You are speaking to God in the Spirit. He is not down playing this dynamic charism, but, by contrasting the purpose of tongues with that of prophecy, he shows that both are good and should not be at odds with each other. In defining tongues this way, he puts more stress on the edification of the assembly than on the individual (vv. 3-4). The term edification is a key word in this chapter. The noun or verb form of the word *edification* is used by Paul only nine times outside the Corinthian letters, yet it is found seven times in 1 Cor. 14 alone. Paul has the corporate vision in mind, not that he is opposed to self-edification, but that it is not of concern here.[72]

Paul greatly desires that they all speak in tongues, but sees the gift of prophecy higher than the gift of tongues. "Now I should like all of you to speak in tongues, but even more to prophesy. One who prophesies is greater than one who speaks in tongues, unless he interprets, so that the church may be built up" (vv. 5-6).

In this passage, it seems that Paul is talking about the gift of prophetic tongues; in which case, a person speaks in a tongue but the interpretation (and sometimes a translation) is spoken in the vernacular. Thus, the message from the Lord is coherent and understandable. This "speaking" can be either glossolalic (unintelligible speech) or xenolalic (known human foreign language). It is not as valuable as prophecy spoken in the vernacular (native language), because no one can understand it without an interpretation. If someone interprets the tongues, then the gift of speaking in tongues has a different role to play, only because now it edifies the congregation. The charism of interpretation of tongues will be discussed in more detail in the section about the types of tongues.

Here, Paul wants to drive home the importance of being intelligible in the assembly. In verses 6-12 he uses three simple and logical arguments to show that sound without intelligibility contributes nothing to the building up of the community:

1. Paul's own ministry:

"Now, brothers if I come to you speaking in tongues, how will I benefit you unless I speak to you in some revelation or knowledge or prophecy or teaching (v. 6)?" Paul, like anyone else, wants and needs to be understood when proclaiming the gospel. C.K. Barret says of this verse, "All these activities. . .(revelations, knowledge, and teaching) are of advantage to the Christian assembly but, without them, speaking in tongues as far as the assembly is concerned is sheer sound, signifying nothing."[73]

2. Musical instruments:

"It is the same way with lifeless instruments which produce sound, such as a flute or a harp. If they do not give the distinct notes, how will anyone know what is being played (v. 7)?" In this instance, Paul uses an obvious example of distinguishing between just noise and intelligible musical notes.

3. Foreign languages:

"If then I do not know the meaning of a sound, I will be a foreigner to the speaker and the speaker a foreigner to me" (v. 11). In foreign languages both parties must understand one another in order to communicate, otherwise they would be talking into the air.

Paul concludes the argument by returning to his main concern which is the Church (v. 12). He wants to make sure that the way the Corinthian glossolalists are using the gift of tongues will not destroy the unity of the community. He then proceeds to explain the fruitfulness of speaking in tongues when exercised in combination with the gift of interpretation (inclusion of the mind which makes the words intelligible).[74]

Paul distinguishes different gifts within the charism of tongues: praying, singing, and speaking. Even though Paul interchanges the words "praying" and "speaking" when describing tongues, he does show that there is a difference because of the emphasis on the gift of interpretation. Speaking in tongues is, more often than not, a message from God given in tongues. Paul knows the power of a revelation, teaching or prophecy given in tongues, and he does not want the one speaking in tongues to waste the message. It needs to be given to the community, thus the gift of interpretation of tongues converts the tongues into a revelation, prophecy, knowledge or teaching and provides edification for the others. In verses 13-19 Paul gives his instruction on the use of tongues in the assembly:

> Therefore, he who speaks in a tongue should pray for the power to interpret. For if I pray in a tongue, my spirit prays but my mind is unfruitful. What am I to do? I will pray with the spirit and I will pray with the mind also; I will sing with the spirit, and I will sing with the mind also. Otherwise, if you bless with spirit, how can anyone in the position of an outsider [those without gifts] say the "Amen" to your thanksgiving when he does not know what you are saying? For you may give thanks well enough, but the other man is not edified. I thank God that I speak in tongues more than you all; nevertheless, in

the church I would rather speak five words with my mind, in order to instruct others, than ten thousand in a tongue (1 Cor. 14:13-19).

The idea here is that when praying, singing or speaking in tongues (without interpretation) the *person* is being edified spiritually. Paul does not condemn personal edification, he promotes it. But again, in this passage he has the good of the community in mind. If a person is going to use the gift of tongues, Paul recommends that for the sake of the assembly the person should desire to include the mind in praying and singing to the Lord (v. 15).

In Paul's example about the advantage of using both the spirit and the mind in the church, he uses the word unbeliever (v. 16) to describe the outsider (RSV: "him that is without gifts"), who cannot say "Amen" when tongues are spoken without an interpretation. B.C. Johanson believes that Paul's mention of the word "position" in verse 16 widens his argument to include not only believers, but proselytes or catechumens for whom prophecy would have more value than tongues.

Paul shows that it is good when a person speaks in tongues because "thanks' are surely given to God. But, it has little benefit if the non-Christian or a Christian who may desire to have more faith, cannot understand what is being proclaimed (v. 17). He then gives witness to his own use of tongues (v. 18), by which he says that he is using the gift of tongues far more than the Corinthian glossolalists. Actually, the literal Greek in verse 18 can be rendered that Paul was thanking God with tongues more than the Corinthians, which fits the context of thanking God in tongues. The importance here is that the apostle made frequent use of the gift of tongues as part of his regular prayer life. On account of Paul being more concerned about building up the church, he says that in the assembly he would rather speak a short, intelligible, uplifting statement of faith "to instruct others," rather than rattle off a seemingly endless proclamation in tongues (v. 19).

Tongues as a Sign for the Unbeliever

After Paul addresses the relationship of tongues and prophecy in the setting of a worship service, he presents these two charisms in the arena of an apostolate in the church — evangelizing others. He quotes from Isaiah 28:11 which compares tongues to foreign speech, and then he proceeds to use this comparison to instruct the Corinthians in the use of tongues and prophecy in the presence of new converts or uninitiated.

Verses 20-25 have been the subject of several conflicting commentaries by biblical scholars. There has been many different opinions and theories about what Paul's meaning is here. The problem centers around the words *unbelievers* and *believers* in verse 22, and by the example Paul gives in verses 23-25:

v. 22. "Thus, tongues are a sign not for believers but for unbelievers, while prophecy is not for unbelievers but for believers.

v. 23. If therefore, the whole church assembles and all speak in tongues, and outsiders or unbelievers enter, will they not say you are mad?

v. 24. But if all prophesy, and an unbeliever or outsider enters, he is convicted by all, he is called to account by all,

v. 25. the secrets of his heart are disclosed; and so falling on his face, he will worship God and declare that God is really among you."

It appears that there is a contradiction with the statement "tongues are a sign not for believers but for unbelievers," because Paul then says that if unbelievers hear tongues they will think the tongue speakers are mad. But if tongues *are* a "sign" for unbelievers why would Paul then say that tongues will not help the unbeliever believe? And if prophecy is a "sign" for the believers and not unbelievers, why does Paul write that when an unbeliever hears prophecy he or she will be converted?

Some bible scholars believe Paul misplaced the words *unbelievers* and *believers*. Others believe it was a copyist's error. J.B. Phillips, in his translation of the Bible, has gone so far as to reverse the two words in order to make better sense of the passage.[75] B.C. Johanson believes Paul is asking a rhetorical question and says that 1 Cor. 14:22 should be rendered, "Are tongues, thus, a sign for unbelievers, and not believers?" (implying that Paul is thinking in the opposite of his question). In other words, Johanson's version has Paul thinking that tongues are a sign for believers, not unbeliev-ers.[76] And there are still others who try to focus on the "sign" value of tongues: If the charism of tongues is a sign, is it a positive or negative sign?

Dr. Scott Hahn, Biblical professor at the University of Steubenville in Ohio believes the key to a legitimate inter-pretation of 1 Cor. 14:22 is the phrase from Isaiah 28:11 which Paul quotes in verse 21. Whenever Paul quoted an Old Testa-ment text, he presumed that the reader either knew the full context of the wording or would refer to the scriptures for its meaning.[77] The text that Paul cites from Isaiah gives us a backdrop for his description of tongues as being a sign for the unbeliever.

In verse 20, he interjects some words of encouragement and advice to his beloved Corinthians. "Brethren, do not be children in your thinking; be babes in evil, but in thinking be mature." In other words, do not boast over your gifts, espe-cially tongues and prophecy. Be humble and use common sense. Why? Paul reminds them, especially the leaders, that the ancient kingdom of Israel had many gifts but, because of pride, the people lost faith in the covenant and in the Lord. By quoting the Scripture Paul makes his point, "...By men of strange tongues and by lips of foreigners will I speak to this people, and even then they will not listen to me, says the Lord" (v. 21).

Paul also writes in verse 21, "in the law it is written...." Hahn and other scholars believe he is referring to

Deuteronomy 28:49, but he actually quotes Isaiah 28:11.[78]
Deutoeronomy 28 contains lists of blessings and curses
spoken by Moses to the people: If they keep the covenant of
the Lord, they will be blessed. If they persist in their pride
and unbelief, the curses will come in the form of plagues,
drought, famine, and conquest. One of the signs of a lack of
faith that Paul is alluding to is the conquest by a people whose
language the Israelites do not understand — the men of strange
tongues.

Isaiah connects the sign of unknown tongues to the unbelieving leaders of Israel. In chapter twenty-eight, he begins
with heated accusations against the king, his royal house, the
priests, and the prophets of Israel who are abusing their many
gifts given by God. They are proud, pompous, and drunk not
only with wine but with power and riches (Is. 28:1-8). They
were given many gifts to build up the people of God in Israel
but their pride kept them from serving the people with their
"charisms." Isaiah promises judgment by the Lord, but not
without a sign. The sign will remind the leaders and the people
of their unbelief. The sign will be the word of the Lord
spoken in a language they will not know. "To whom will he
impart knowledge and to whom will he explain the message?
Those just weaned from milk, those taken from the breast?
For he says: "Sau Lasau Cau Lacau Ze'er Sham Ze'er Sham"
(Is. 28:9-10).[79] Verse 10 is very difficult to translate. In fact,
translators do not know the exact meaning. It is comparable
to childish babble — "goo-goo, gaa-gaa" or "la la la la la."[80]
It does not make sense, which is exactly the prophet's point.

And, this is also Paul's point. Tongues is the word of the Lord but the language is not intelligible. And Paul does not want a gift of God to be a source of pride and fall from grace simply because of an immature use of it.

Isaiah continues by saying that the word of the Lord will be proclaimed but if the anointed ones — the king, the prophet, and the priest are not receiving God's word, who will? Perhaps the infants are the only ones worthy to receive the word of the Lord.[81] The next verse (v. 12) is the passage that Paul quotes in 1 Corinthians: "Nay, but men of strange lips and with alien tongue the Lord will speak to this people to whom he said: 'This is the resting place, give rest to the weary; here is repose;' yet they would not listen. So for them the word of the Lord shall be: *Sau Lasau Cau Lacau Ze'er Sham Ze'er Sham*, that they may go; fall backward and be broken and snared and captured" (Is. 28:11-13).

The alien tongue will be a sign to the unbelieving Israelites that God has pronounced judgment against their lack of faith and sinful pride, which has brought hardship, division, and even death. This reality was understood when the Assyrian army, in 722 B.C., swept down from the north, annihilated the ten tribes of Israel and nearly destroyed the Kingdom of Judah and Jerusalem. (2 Kings 18-19). But this judgment, like all judgments of God, was meant to be medicinal. It was needed to awaken a faith that was lost.

A few verses later, Isaiah gives a prophecy (v. 28:16) about the restoration of Israel. He identifies the "precious cornerstone" as the Messiah This passage is quoted frequently in the New Testament because it denotes a type of resurrection. The strange tongues are a preparation for judgment on an unbelieving generation. However, what follows when the people receive the word of God in faith, is the hope of healing and restoration.[82]

Paul uses this Scripture text to warn the glossolalists in Corinth not to become proud about their gift of tongues because the presence of strange tongues are a sign for unbelievers. Unknown tongues have been used as a sign by God to expose unbelief, not only for nations (Dt. 28:49 and Is. 28:11), but this can be for individuals in the churches as well. Paul wants them to realize that this charism of tongues is a gift of the Holy Spirit and that they must be careful not to fall into unbelief just as the people of Israel had.

Since the gift of tongues is subordinate to the gift of prophecy, Paul wants the tongue speakers of Corinth to yield to the prophets who will in turn speak the word of God. If they do not, he warns them, the spoken word of God will become unintelligible and bring judgment upon them in the same way as it did in Isaiah's time.

The Corinthians prided themselves on tongues as sign of favor; a means of direct communication with God. To challenge them to a more mature appraisal, Paul draws from Scripture a less flattering explanation of what speaking in tongues may signify. Equating tongues with foreign languages (1 Cor. 14:10-11), Paul concludes from Isaiah that tongues is a sign, not for those who believe; that is, not a mark of God's pleasure for those who listen to Him, but a mark of His displeasure with those in the community who are faithless and who have not heeded the message that He has sent through the prophets.[83]

Paul expects them to understand his example from Isaiah and wants them to see that their own boasting and selfishness takes away their child-like faith. The word of the Lord will still be pronounced but, will they accept it in faith and hear it proclaimed clearly, or in their unbelief, will the word of the Lord be foreign to them; no better than childish babble? "Be babes in evil, but in thinking be mature" (1 Cor. 14:20).

Realizing this background from Is. 28:11, Paul then states, "Thus, tongues are a sign not for believers, but for unbelievers, while prophecy is not for unbelievers but for believers" (v. 22). Paul is convinced that the charism of tongues is a sign from God for unbelievers or someone who lacks faith. But what kind of sign, a good one or bad? It depends. Tongues can be a positive sign or a negative sign according to the disposition of the unbeliever. Tongues alone does not bring faith, it needs help. This could possibly be one of the contentions between the glossolalists and the prophets in the Corinthian church; tongues being seen as the prominent sign to bring or build faith.

Again, Paul is not giving an exhaustive teaching on tongues but a biblical interpretation. In the gospel of Mark, Jesus calls tongues one of the "signs" that will be present in the believers. It would appear that Paul is focusing on some of the aspects of the gift of tongues, but not all, even though the apostle describes this gift quite well. Paul is talking about tongues being a sign for the unbeliever, while in Mark tongues are a sign in or that accompany the believer. Tongues alone does not produce faith in the believer, but can demonstrate the power faith can bring.

Paul illustrates what may happen when an unbeliever or possibly a catechumen enters the assembly. "If all speak in tongues and outsiders or unbelievers enter, will they not say you are mad?" (v. 23). Why does Paul think unbelievers will have this reaction? What point is Paul trying to make? Not only is Paul using the Old Testament background but he could be referencing the event of the descent of the Holy Spirit at Pentecost. When the Twelve Apostles and others, including the Virgin Mary, received the Holy Spirit and spoke in tongues (Acts 2:1-4), the reaction of those who heard them was one of bewilderment. "And at this sound the multitude came together, and they were bewildered. …And they were amazed and wondered" (Acts 2:6-7).

Devout Jews in Jerusalem from every nation under heaven heard the words of God, "…We hear them telling in our own tongues the mighty works of God" (Acts 2:11). Did they suddenly find faith in Jesus of Nazareth when they heard the tongues alone? The multitude of Jews did hear in their own languages but they also must have heard the other languages as well, or at least realized that others were hearing in their own languages. Nevertheless, the response to the Apostles was not one of faith. "And all were amazed and perplexed, saying to one another, 'What does this mean?' But others mocking said, 'They are filled with new wine'" (Acts 2:12-13).

So when the Apostles spoke in tongues at Pentecost it produced confusion for the hearers and some thought they were drunk. It was unsettling, possibly to the point of appearing mad.[84] To the ones manifesting the tongues, it was a gift of prayer and proclamation; it was not a sign for them as believers to give them faith, but a gift of praise that demonstrated their faith. For the others, the gift of tongues was a sign to bring their unbelief to the surface (remember, the multitude knew of Jesus and what He had accomplished, Acts 2:22). This sign also primed the people to hear the word of God made flesh in Jesus the Christ, who had recently risen from the dead. Only when Peter preached and prophesied to the crowds did they begin to understand this sign of tongues. However, an interpretation was needed in order for the sign to bring them faith (Acts 2:14).

Thus, this sign of tongues was a positive sign for the unbeliever seeking faith and a negative one for the unbeliever who is not seeking faith. When prophecy is proclaimed the unbeliever can enter into the dimension of faith in Christ and understand the good news of the resurrection with child-like faith. And, is it a coincidence that after his teaching on tongues and prophecy Paul begins to speak about the resurrection, which is the longest part of his letter? (1 Cor. 15). Peter's interpretation of the tongues is a support of Paul's point. Paul is not interested in simply exposing unbelief, but instilling faith. The sign value of "prophecy is not for unbelievers, but for believers" (v. 22). Paul's point is clear. When believers hear a prophecy in their native language, it will edify their faith more than tongues that are unintelligible. (v. 2).

In the illustration of the unbeliever entering the assembly, Paul demonstrates the contrast between the charism of tongues and prophecy; showing the superiority of prophecy to bring faith (1 Cor. 14:23-25). Prophecy does not only do this, but aids the gift of speaking in tongues to become a sign for unbelievers to receive faith through the gift of interpretation of tongues (v. 26-27). Tongues may very well prepare one to hear the "good news," but prophecy is needed as well to be the sign for someone who wishes to believe. Paul wants to drive home the point that even though the gift of tongues is a charism of the Holy Spirit it does not produce faith on its own. It may very well be an edifying experience to one using the gift and even as a community harmonizing in the spirit as a gift of prayer, but it will not edify or bring lasting faith to another because it is unintelligible, and faith comes through hearing and understanding (Rom. 10:17).

Paul's warning to the glossolalists is for them not to profess that tongues is the prominent gift to produce faith. If they do, then this gift of the Holy Spirit will become a sign of judgment for them; eventually producing unbelief, division, and possibly spiritual death to the community.

Good Order in the Liturgy

Paul leads us to believe that the liturgies and the settings for worship or prayer meetings in the church of Corinth were not boring by any means. In fact, there was so much activity happening that Paul had to set some serious guidelines to regulate the community toward the edification of all and not just for the individual. In vv. 26-33, Paul lays down guidelines to point out that just because a person is gifted in a certain charism, it did not include the right to impose it upon the whole community in a disorderly fashion. "When you come together, one has a hymn, another a teaching, or a revelation; one speaks in a tongue, or interprets. Let all things be done for edification" (v. 26).

It is important to show what Paul permits as well as what he does not. William Richardson believes that "...In view of the disorder described in v. 26, it is significant that the expressive, outspoken Paul opts for regulation instead of prohibition in v. 27. Paul proceeds with instructions on how the gift is to be practiced and liturgical order preserved. Apparently, for Paul, orderly control was not in opposition to the free and open operation of the Spirit. But in v. 28, he states that if there is no one to interpret, then the person who speaks in tongues should keep silent, speaking only to oneself or to God."[85]

Paul's main thrust is missionary, and with the extreme events happening in the Corinthian church he wants to make sure there are no elements that would repel any outsiders or unbelievers.

Paul neither discourages the private use of tongues (even when it is not building up the church directly) nor does he believe that speaking in tongues is a self-addressed delusion. It is an authentic gift of the Holy Spirit but should be exercised in public with order.[86]

The Gift of Prophecy

Even though it would appear that Paul has given the upper-hand to the prophets, he does lay down some rules for the ones who have received the gift of prophecy. Paul sets limits on the number of prophets who can speak in the assembly; in this way the assembly's gift of discerning spirits (1 Cor. 12:10), not just the charism of the prophecy will be exercised (1 Cor. 14: 29). Stressing order in the assembly, Paul recommends that the prophets should speak their prophecy one at a time. If done in this manner, everyone present can learn and be uplifted (v. 30). Barret states, "It is clear that the Spirit now wishes to communicate a fresh truth through a different speaker...It is implied that the prophets, though inspired, are able to control their speech."[87] The same can be said of the ones who pray or speak in tongues.

When Paul uses the Greek word *pantes* (meaning *all*) in

v. 31, it would seem that he is referring to each instance of prophecy: "You can all speak your prophecies, but one by one, so all may be instructed or encouraged." He does not assert that all Christians will necessarily take part in the activity — technically described as prophesying — only that all may do so. It is not any human decision that makes a person a prophet, or prevents someone from being a prophet. The action of prophecy is solely inspired within the freedom of the Holy Spirit, and in this context, prophecy is shown to be a function and not an office.

With an understanding that it is the Holy Spirit who activates the gift of prophecy, Paul also makes sure that he covers the practical aspects of exercising the gift. In reference to liturgies and prayer meetings, he adamantly states that "...the spirit of the prophet is under the prophet's control, since God is a God, not of confusion, but of peace" (1 Cor. 14: 32-33). Most probably, he wrote this so the prophet would not have a reason, as some in Corinth may have argued, to continue speaking because "the Spirit inspired" the prophet to do so; if there is a reason for silence then the prophet should keep silent. This restrictive view was expressed by Paul because of abuse of the gift of prophecy. And the opposite case of someone receiving a prophecy and not proclaiming it to the assembly, because of fear or uncertainty, also would show that once a prophecy is given it is under the control of the prophet. God is not manifested by disorder but by peace.

In concluding his teaching on tongues and prophecy, Paul really is serious about not abusing the gifts of the Holy Spirit and refers to the authority of his apostleship as "a command of the Lord" (v. 37). If people disassociate themselves from this command to do their own will, they should not be recognized (v. 38). The apostle's concluding statement is similar to his opening one in v. 1, about desiring the gift of prophecy and allowing the gift of tongues to be used in worship. "So, my brethren, earnestly desire to prophesy, and do not forbid speaking in tongues; but all things should be done decently and in order" (v. 39-40).

Learning from the Corinthian Experience

It would certainly seem that the Corinthian church was a unique one. Unfortunately, it often lacked the ability to sustain an atmosphere of loving, spiritual worship. Fortunately, for the succeeding ages and ourselves, Paul responded not only by correcting but in giving instruction through true apostolic love. We would not have such an extensive scriptural teaching on communal worship (the Eucharistic liturgy and prayer meetings), if the Corinthians had not been abusive in using the gifts. They were zealous and this probably inspired Paul, who knew about zeal for God, to put so much energy into the formation of their community. The use of the charisms is an important part of living out the Christian faith and, should be promoted because they are gifts given by the Spirit of Christ for the common good.

What St. Paul taught, the Church now develops and teaches; namely, that the charisms should be used dutifully for the edification of the faithful. And, those who preside over the Church have the right and the responsibility to judge the authenticity and proper use of the charisms.

It would be ideal if the pastor could lead his parish prayer group meetings, but if not, proper pastoral guidance and direction from lay leaders is still very important. The ones exercising the gifts should recognize the authority and role of the Church leaders and remember the reasons behind the manifestations of the charisms, especially prophecy and tongues. Paul desired to reflect the image of Jesus Christ and saw this in striving for love. He tirelessly taught the precepts of love and hoped that Christians would make love their aim and earnestly desire the spiritual gifts.

THE CHARISM OF TONGUES IN THE HISTORY OF THE CHURCH

The charism of tongues has been in use throughout the history of the Church. It has received more attention in the last thirty years because of its widespread manifestation in both Catholic and non-Catholic churches, and also through the Charismatic Renewal. In some eras of Christian history tongues was quite common as a gift of prayer and edification, and in other eras it seemed to be dormant, although not extinct.

The Post-Apostolic Era

One may wonder why the fathers of post-apostolic times did not write more about this charism. Possibly, little was written about tongues because the early Church had to deal with more important issues. For instance, it was a difficult task to present "the faith" as reasonable while, at the same time, trying to eliminate false accusations about Christians. If the charism of tongues had been promoted it would "…have added fuel to the fire that flamed into irrational rejection of Christians as monsters or, at best, queer people."[88]

Another thought on why the charism of tongues was not extensively written about could be that these early Christian writers concentrated more on the source of the gifts than on the gifts themselves (the nature of Christ, the Trinity, and the function of the Holy Spirit). However, there were several early writers who did acknowledge the existence and credibility of the charism of tongues.

St. Irenaeus (140-202), an apostolic father and bishop of Lyons, discussed tongues as a prophetic gift. In his commentary on the Baptism of Cornelius by Peter in Acts, he wrote: "Neither for a like reason, would he [Peter] have given them Baptism so readily, had he not heard them prophesying when the Holy Spirit rested upon them."[89]

According to Kelsey, Irenaeus knew what he was talking about. In his work, *Against Heresies*, Irenaeus mentions the gift of knowing "all languages," and uttering "prophetic expressions," which gives witness to the existence of tongues in his day.[90]

Tertullian (150-230), the great Christian scholar, mentions the charism of tongues as a sign of authenticity for the Church. He also draws attention to his own personal experience; placing the charism of tongues in the realm of prophetic utterances. In *Tertullian Against Marcion*, he wrote:

> Let Marcion then exhibit, as gifts of his God, some prophets, such as have not spoken by human sense, but with the Spirit of God, such as have both predicted things to come, and have made manifest the secrets of the heart (1 Cor. 14:25); let him produce a psalm, a vision, a prayer — only let it be by the Spirit, in an ecstasy, that is, a rapture, whenever an interpretation of tongues has occurred to him. ...Now all these signs are forthcoming from my side without any difficulty, and they agree, too, with the rules, and the dispensations, and the instructions of the Creator; therefore without doubt the Christ, and the Spirit, and the apostle, belong severally to my God. Here, then, is my frank avowal for any one who cares to require it.[91]

When discussing Tertullian, the topic of Montanism necessarily arises. This movement, which began in the early third century as a renewal of the Church in the Spirit, resulted in an abuse of the charisms. Towards the latter part of his life, Tertullian incorporated many ways of the Montanists into his spirituality. Montanus claimed that the Holy Spirit resided in him, in a special way, to purify the Church. He and his co-leaders (who were prophetesses), and their followers placed an undue importance on the charismatic gifts of tongues and prophecy and practiced a life of austerity. The Montanists eventually would not accept the full authority of the Church and the movement separated into schism. The problem was not in the demonstration of the spiritual charisms, but in the fact that Montanus set up a rival charismatic hierarchy against that of the Church.[92] These gifts eventually became associated with Montanism and, as the movement died out, the charism of tongues seemed to be emphasized less.

Since Tertullian seems to be the last Western father in this age to discuss the charism of tongues, we turn our attention to the East. Origen (185-250), a priest who was a prolific writer on scripture and spiritual matters, lived in Egypt and Palestine. He held two notions with respect to the charism of tongues. First he believed that the gift of speaking in tongues was the same as speaking the languages of the nations. "In this particular instance Origen's understanding of the gift of tongues appears to have been an example of xenolalia, defined in this case as an ability given by God through the grace of the Holy Spirit to bridge the language barrier for the purpose of cross-cultural preaching."[93] As with most of the fathers before him, Origen seemed to explain the gift of tongues in the prophetic sense which included the gift of interpretation. And he believed that when the one preaching learned the new language the charism ended.[94]

Origen's other viewpoint about tongues was that this charism is a valid form of prayer. He links praying in the Spirit, as referenced in Romans 8:28, explicitly with praying in tongues.[95]

It is impossible to know from the text whether or not tongues in this form of prayer should be understood as xenolalic in form, or whether it should be taken as true glos-solalia. What is known, however, is that Origen must have held that praying in tongues existed in his day, and it was thought to be beneficial in that it was through this type of prayer that the Spirit interceded exceedingly before God.[96]

As for tongues in a public prayer service or liturgy, Origen follows Paul's direction closely. The one who speaks in a tongue speaks to God, and an uninterpreted tongue is not edifying to the ones present. It is necessary for the tongues to be interpreted.[97]

This period also witnessed the rise of desert monasticism. Monks known as Hesecastic desert monks were known to practice a form of prayer that used tongues to move them into deep, contemplative union with God. Hampsch relates that the monks, either in two's or three's, would begin to pray "in a language not their own" and would continue to pray this way; eventually the Spirit brought them into such a high state of contemplation that they would be "utterly silent at the experience of God."[98]

The Post-Nicene Era

In the period after the Council of Nicea in 325, from the early fourth century into the early middle ages, the charism of tongues was viewed strictly as an apostolic gift. A large percentage of writers believed this charism only resembled the gift given at Pentecost. Speaking in tongues in a foreign language (xenolalia), or even prophetic tongues, was only given for purposes of evangelization. Since Christianity was growing rapidly in the Roman Empire at this time, most felt that this gift was no longer needed in spreading the faith.

In a sense they were right, but another aspect of this charism was highly promoted and written about, even if there was not a direct mention of its connection with tongues. This aspect of the charism of tongues is called "jubilation." The word jubilation comes from the Latin word *jubilatio* which means shouting loudly or whooping.[99]

Basically jubilation describes expressions of rejoicing praise to God, either in song, dance, or vocal prayer. Although there was jubilation in the vernacular and also in bodily motions, there was also jubilation that had the same qualities as the gift of singing or praying in tongues, similar to the description given by St. Paul in his first letter to the Corinthians. Jubilation in this form is described as a wordless song or prayer of rejoicing offered to God. It seemed to be a common way of praying from the heart when words could not manifest the experience of the worshiper.[100] In Part III, jubilation in tongues will be discussed further.

There were many pastors during this period of the Church who recognized this gift and strongly encouraged the faithful to engage in this type of worship in private prayer and in liturgy. St. Augustine was probably the most famous of these.

Augustine, in *Vera Religioni*, believed that the charismatic gifts were given to the apostolic Church to help the Church in its beginning. Subsequently the miracles of the apostles were not to last to his day. The gift of speaking in tongues was a miracle of the apostles, and Augustine was not too interested in the furthering of this gift. However, he later recanted his statement about miracles and added: "For, when I wrote that book, I myself had recently learned that a blind man had been restored to sight in Milan near the bodies of the martyrs in that very city, and I knew about some others, so numerous even in these times, that we cannot know about all of them nor enumerate those we know."[101] It would appear that Augustine was trying to keep people from longing for the nostalgia of apostolic times and from wishing for apostolic miracles. Instead he wanted to keep his flock focused on edifying each other. In this he realized he had gone to an extreme and reclarified his previous statement, especially after he became not only an eyewitness to miraculous healings, but an instrument as well.

Having altered his belief on miracles, what does Augustine say about the charism of tongues? He seems very clear about one aspect of the charism of tongues, "speaking in tongues" or prophetic tongues; this gift given to the apostles at Pentecost was viewed by some in Augustine's time as a special apostolic gift for evangelizing, and since it would appear that the known world was becoming Christian, Augustine may have reasoned that this gift was no longer needed.[102]

Augustine makes such statements as: "These signs were adapted to the time. For there behooved to be betokening of the Holy Spirit in all tongues, to show that the Gospel of God was to run through all tongues over the whole earth. That thing was done for a betokening, and it passed away."[103] And he says further, "For who expects in these days that those on whom hands are laid that they may receive the Holy Spirit should forthwith begin to speak in tongues?"[104]

Augustine's opinion may have been extreme because he may not have experienced this gift as it was in the apostolic Church. As mentioned previously, there are various types of the charism of tongues, and prophetic tongues for evangelization was apparently unheard of in Augustine's society because Christianity by that time was largely accepted and there was a common language throughout the Roman empire.

Augustine does seem to be familiar with another type of the charism of tongues called jubilation in tongues. He may not have called it tongues, but the characteristics of it are there because jubilation was well known to Augustine. This form of singing and praying aloud without words was very common and was used frequently in liturgical celebrations. Augustine, in his *Commentary on the Psalms*, says, "Where speech does not suffice…they break into singing on vowel sounds, that through this means the feeling of the soul may be expressed, words fail to explain the heart's conceptions. Therefore, if they jubilate from earthly exhilarations, should we not sing jubilation out of heavenly, singing what words cannot express."[105]

And again, Augustine speaks of the spontaneity and word-lessness of jubilation: "He who sings a jubilus does not utter words; he pronounces a wordless sound of joy...he simply lets his joy burst forth without words; his voice then appears to express a happiness so intense that he cannot formulate it."[106]

One last example from Augustine shows the general acceptance of this charism by his congregation and the power of this gift of the spirit. Augustine tells of two miraculous healings that happened during the Easter season. Recorded in his work *The City of God*, he describes a young brother and sister, Paulinus and Palladia, who both had a disorder that caused trembling and convulsions. By way of a dream, they were inspired to come to Hippo to pray at the shrine of the martyr, St. Stephen. At the Easter morning liturgy, Paulinus fell into a convulsion against the railing of the shrine and was instantly healed: "Then everyone burst into a prayer of thankfulness to God. The entire church rang with clamor of rejoicing." The bishop then embraced the youth and kissed him.

The very next day the same healing was experienced by Palladia, and the response was no different: "Such a wonder rose up from men and women together that the exclamations and tears seemed as if they would never come to an end. ...The people shouted God's praises without words, but with such a noise that our ears could scarcely stand it. What was there in the hearts of all this clamoring crowd but the faith of Christ, for which St. Stephen shed his blood?[107]

There are other Church fathers in this time period who described tongues in ways similar to Augustine's. The Patriarch of Constantinople, St. John Chrysostom, did not know what to make of tongues, like many of his contemporaries, but knew of the jubilation gift. St. Ambrose, St. Jerome, St. Cassian, St. Peter Chrysologus, and St. Gregory the Great also speak of jubilation. In short, most of the major Christian thinkers in the Roman Empire and the early Middles Ages knew about and promoted this gift.[108] Again, they did not call it "the gift of tongues," but it bares a striking resemblance to this charism in the realm of private prayer and liturgical worship.

Another interesting character of the later patristic period is Marcus Auerli Cassiodori. He was a monk who lived near Rome in the sixth century. He was an educator in both sacred and secular subjects. He wrote a massive commentary on the Psalms, where he mentions jubilation some eight or ten times.[109] For him, "Jubilation is called an exultation of the heart, which, because it is such an infinite joy, cannot be explained in words." And again, "Jubilation with great delight leaps with joy into the voice. What the speech of a confused voice cannot explain, the devout bursting forth of the rejoicing believer declares." [110] St. Isidore of Seville, a doctor of the Church, who lived in the sixth and seventh centuries commented on this spiritual gift of jubilation. He says, "Language cannot explain...words cannot explain. ...It is an effusion of the soul. …When the joy of exultation erupts by means of the voice, this is known as jubilation."[111]

The Middle Ages

The Church of the Middle Ages basically followed the lead of the early Church fathers and used the same terminology in referring to tongues. They viewed the charism of tongues as xenolalia for apostolic or missionary preaching. They saw its significance as a gift of the Holy Spirit that gave the preacher the gift of communicating with people who did not understand the preacher's native language. They also recognized the gift of tongues in jubilation and had much to say about this. This section will give overviews of both aspects of the charism of tongues.

The people of the Medieval period were great believers in miracles and in the power of Christ working through the Church. The gift of tongues, as well as other pneumatic charisms, were expected to happen through people who had a reputation for holiness. The gift of jubilation, in particular, was a well-known and non-controversial expression of prayer, and it seemed to have been used quite often.[112] There is evidence of this in religious orders. St. Romuald, the founder of the Camaldolese monks in the eleventh century, is said to have received the "tongues of angels" before he died. It was associated with the Cistercian traditions, especially through the writings and preaching of St. Bernard of Clairvaux, and with the early Franciscan communities, based on the gift of jubilation that St. Francis possessed. This age was marked by renewal and revival in the faith of Christ, and the gift of jubilation was one of the vehicles the Holy Spirit used to inspire the people of God to worship. In *Sounds of Wonder*, E. Ensely comments that in early Franciscan literature actual sounds of certain jubilations are written out, and these descriptions are strikingly similar to descriptions of modern day glossolalia in the Charismatic Renewal.[113]

Jacopone da Todi (1228-1306), a Franciscan and mystical writer and poet, describes jubilation in ways similar to that of modern charismatics, describing glossolalia in his poem, *Of the Jubilus of the Heart*:

> *The Jubilus in fire awakes*
> *And straight the man must sing and pray,*
> *His tongue in childish stammering shakes,*
> *Nor knows he what his lips may say;*
> *He can not hide or quench away*
> *That Sweet pure and infinite...*
> *...And see! his neighbor stand apart,*
> *and mock the senseless chatter;*
> *They deem his speech a foolish blur,*
> *A shadow of his spirit's light.*[114]

Even in the Scholastic tradition jubilation was well known, mainly because Scholastic writers were carrying on the traditions of the early fathers. St. Thomas Aquinas, the great Scholastic theologian of the thirteenth century, describes jubilation as "...an unspeakable joy, which cannot be expressed.

The reason that this joy cannot be expressed in words is that it is beyond comprehension. . . . Such is the goodness of God that it cannot be expressed and even if it could be expressed, it could only imperfectly be expressed."[115] Other theologians in this period, such as St. Albert the Great, St. Bonaventure, Jean Gerson, and Peter Lombard, speak of jubilation in similar ways.[116]

The next two centuries witnessed an increased number of mystical writers from various parts of Europe. These writers covered many areas of prayer and union with God, and it seemed that "jubilation" was frequently discussed. People like Blessed John Ruysbroeck, Blessed Henry Suso, and Blessed Richard Rolle, all of whom lived in the fourteenth century, mention jubilation many times. Ruysbroeck, who was the Dutch founder of a lay religious movement and of the Canons Regular of St. Augustine, calls jubilation "a joy that cannot be uttered in words" that sometimes causes a person "to break out into shouting whilst he is being spiritually touched or pricked."[117] Henry Suso speaks similarly of jubilation as more of an intimate conversation with God: "I had certain tender conversations with my Creator in which only my spirit talked. I wept and sighed; I laughed and cried."[118]

Richard Rolle, an English mystic, writer and hermit, probably explored the depths of the gift of jubilation more than anyone else. His writings are not well known in our century, but some compare them to those of St. Teresa of Avila and St. Bernard of Clairvaux. He had a tremendous gift for spontaneously inspired songs and received many mystical experiences while singing and praying in jubilation. He once said of jubilation, "That wonderful praise is on the soul, and for abundance of joy and sweetness it ascends into the mouth so that the heart and tongue accord as one, and the body and soul rejoice, living in God." He so pierced the depths of this type of praise that he often went into rapture while singing. "Hence he sings his prayers to God, in a wonderful and indescribable way, because, just as now the heavenly sound descends his spirit, so also, ascending in a superabundance of joy to his mouth, the same sound is heard."[119] Although he had this gift for inspired prayer in his own language, it would appear that he also engaged in the wordless praise of jubilation as the Spirit moved him.

Among common believers, there is evidence of great faith and charismatic elements in the realm of communal prayer. Ensely states that there are many references to jubilation as a seemingly normal way of expressing praise to God in liturgy. "One finds many examples of groups and congregations breaking into spontaneous worship in the midst of liturgical services."[120] The prayer of jubilation was eventually incorporated into the liturgy at a set time before the gospel was read and after the "Alleluia." The assembly was invited to extend the singing of the "Alleluia" through more spontaneous praise in the form of wordless jubilation, shouting loudly. This praise could last for up to twenty minutes. In some parts of central Europe this remained as part of the official liturgy in local Catholic churches until the sixteenth century.[121]

The experience of tongues in the form of jubilation was very evident to the Church of the Middle ages as a gift of prayer for the edification of the individual and of the assembly. The charism of tongues was viewed also as a valid expression of edification for the Church in its work of preaching and evangelization. There are actual accounts of xenolalia happening in missionary activity, as reports about the preaching ministries of the saints began surfacing at this time.

Fernando de Bouillon of Lisbon, Portugal, who became St. Anthony the Wonder-Worker of Padua, (1195-1231), was known for his brilliant and poetic sermons. He traveled to many regions in Italy and France. This missionary of the Franciscan Order exhibited great power that confirmed his preaching through miracles, healings, the gift of prophetic speech and speaking in other languages, of which he had no previous knowledge.

> His preaching was nearly always confirmed by miracles; the sermon itself was in some sense miraculous. He must have possessed the gift of tongues. While in Italy he preached in Italian; yet all the knowledge he possessed of that mellifluous tongue he got during his brief intercourse (communication) with the six illiterate lay brothers at the hospice in the solitude of Monte Paolo. While in France he preached in French, though he had never studied the language. Perhaps more remarkable still is the fact that the simple-minded and the most ignorant listeners were capable of fully comprehending all he said; and his voice, though gentle and sweet, was distinctly heard at a very extraordinary distance from the speaker.[122]

St. Dominic Guzman (1180-1215), a Spaniard and founder of the Order of Preachers, was said to have received this gift. One story claims that he obtained instant knowledge of German when having to speak to seminarians in Germany.[123]

St. Vincent Ferrer (1350-1418), another Spanish Domini-
can, was said to have had this gift and through it converted
thousands of people in western Europe. Kelsey comments:

> St. Vincent Ferrer, a native of Valencia, supposedly only spoke
> Limousin, the local dialect. ...He reached and converted people all
> over western Europe, many in isolated areas. He was reported to
> have been understood in the Alpine regions and other parts of
> Switzerland, in Brittany and Flanders, the Savoy and Lyons, by people
> who knew only the local tongue. While in Genoa he spoke to a group
> of men and women of mixed linguistic backgrounds, all of whom
> were said to have heard him in their own languages. He could also
> understand the Bretons in their own dialect. ...Indeed this is the closest
> parallel, in fact or imagination, to the experience of Acts 2 that we
> find recorded.[124]

St. Thomas Aquinas, in his commentary on speaking in
tongues, explains that this gift was given as an aid in evangelization: "Consequently it was necessary, in this respect, that
God should provide them [the Apostles] with the gift of
tongues; in order that, as the diversity of tongues brought
upon the nations when they fell away to idolatry, according
to Gen. XI, so when the nations were to be recalled to worship of one God a remedy to this diversity might be applied
by the gift of tongues.[125]

Paralleling the scriptural teaching of St. Paul, Aquinas
states that prophecy is greater than tongues because the
charism of tongues involves speaking words that only
"signify" a truth, and as such can be compared to an imagi-
nary vision, whereas prophecy involves the direct enlighten-

ment of the intellect and needs no signification.[126]

He also sees tongues as a gift of praise. "He that speaks in a tongue is said to speak not unto men, i.e. to men's understanding or profit, but unto God's understanding and praise."[127] Thomas also comments on the gift of interpreting tongues by saying that this gift is more excellent than the charism of tongues itself because it is on the same level as prophecy; it is listed after tongues in 1 Cor. 12:12, he states, "because the interpretation of tongues extends even to the interpretation of different kinds of tongues."[128]

The 1500's to the Modern Era

In this period of revolt and reformation in the Church, the presence of the charism of tongues was still evident. In this age of great missionary activity, the gift of speaking in tongues in a foreign language was still popularly professed, and the teaching and expression of jubilation remained alive in the Church at this time.

St. Francis Xavier is probably the most well known saint of this era to have used this gift. He "performed many miracles, was granted the gift of tongues...healed countless persons, established churches in remote areas, and is reported to have raised several persons from the dead."[129] After participating in founding the new order of the Society of Jesus, Xavier set out for India and later traveled to Japan and China to preach the Gospel. It is believed that he preached in Spanish but was heard by the people in their native languages. This gift is a nuanced version of xenolalia, similar to that of St.Vincent Ferrer. The anointing seems to have been on the people hearing and not on St. Francis Xavier speaking their native languages. Some historians hold this as not worthy of belief, but there must have been enough foundation in truth to warrant handing on the tradition of his having this gift.

Others who were reported to have manifested xenolalic tongues were St. Mary Magdalene de Pazzi and Christine the Admirable, both of whom were said to have been able to sing and speak in Latin, a language neither of them had learned.[130]

St. Teresa of Jesus (from Avila, Spain), one of the great mystical writers of the sixteenth century, received her theology of jubilation from previous traditions. She often engaged in various types of jubilation — in what appears to have been in tongues, as well as in dance, and in music. Often times with her Carmelite sisters, as part of their liturgical celebrations, she would sing improvised melodies in praise of God, in the jubilation tradition. Sometimes words and even dance were sudden and spontaneous, according to the inspiration of the Spirit.[131]

Teresa describes the supernatural benefit from the manifestation of this charism of praise as one that lifts the soul into the joy of God and is not forgotten but "impressed upon the imagination."[132] This jubilation would at times bring Teresa and her sisters into a form of spiritual inebriation that could last all day.[133] This spiritual inebriation experienced by

Teresa, as Ensely interprets it, has glossolalic characteristics. Teresa says: "Many words are spoken during this state in praise of God, but, unless the Lord himself puts order to them, they have no orderly form. The understanding, at any rate, counts for nothing here; the soul would like to shout praises aloud, for it is in such a state that it cannot contain itself — a state of delectable disquiet. ...O God, what must that soul be like when it is in this state! It would preferably be all tongue, so that it might praise the Lord. It utters a thousand holy follies, striving ever to please him who thus possesses it."[134]

Other saints and spiritual writers who were familiar with jubilation were St. John of the Cross, St. Philip Neri, Dante Alighieri, Martin Luther, and Francis Bacon.[135] Even though they may have not alluded specifically to the charism of tongues in their reflections of jubilation, it is interesting to note that they engaged in and encouraged jubilation as an ardent form of prayer.[136]

In the seventeenth and eighteenth century in the Catholic Church, with the rising fear of heterodoxy and theological energy increasingly being spent on defending orthodoxy, there seemed to be less written about jubilation and tongues. Jansenism, viewed by some at the time as a Catholic holiness movement in France, had characteristics similar to the Montanists in regard to spiritual rigorism and also in manifestation of pneumatic charisms, such as prophecy and tongues.[137]

We also hear of extraordinary phenomenon among Protestant sects like the Huguenots of Cevennol in Southern France, who were said to have exhibited the gifts of prophecy, tongues, visions and apparitions, and to have heard angelic sounds and music. Most of those who received these gifts were children, and they were soon called "the little prophets of Cevenned." Apparently they inspired the whole province and supposedly there were many positive conversions, both morally and spiritually. During this time Catholic France was cruelly persecuting the Huguenots, and the people of the province, listening to these prophecies, took up arms, like the Maccabees in scripture, but were overrun by the French government.[138]

During this time in the Catholic Church, there were some allusions to the charism of tongues. The Benedictine Father Augustine Baker, in his work *Confessions*,[139] writes about receiving what he describes as being very similar to the gift of tongues. And St. Alphonsus Liguori speaks about jubilation.

The charismatic gifts including tongues, prophecy, and healing began to grow in the Protestant movements as well. The traditions that developed came largely from the theology of John Calvin and John Wesley. These movements deal directly with baptism in the Spirit, inner conversion, and the possible signs that accompany these experiences. There are four principal expressions: 1) The Puritans or Reformed Sealers who believe the experience of being sealed in the Spirit guarantees salvation; 2) the Wesleyan and Wesleyan-Holiness movements which see this as a sanctifying event to perfect love; 3) the Keswick movement which views this as an endowment with power for the service of God; and 4) the classic Pentecostal movement, which believes that baptism in the Spirit is manifested only by tongues.[140]

In the nineteenth century, the charism of tongues did not receive much attention and was certainly not present in liturgy. Charismatic occurrences became more and more associated with saintly people rather than with common experience; for example, St. John Vianney is said to have prayed in tongues.[141] More generally, however, this phenomenon became associated with heterodoxy, (beliefs contrary to established doctrines) and even with demonic activity. The gift of tongues and jubilation seemed to disappear from liturgical worship and may only have been manifested in the lives of individuals or small groups outside of liturgy.

Early in the twentieth century, non-Catholic Pentecostal Movements began to grow, especially in the United States. The charism of tongues was very prevalent in these church services, which centered on the Bible and emphasized the classical charisms of 1 Cor. 12:8-11. It sometimes appeared to be sheer emotionalism when spontaneous prayer would occur in these gatherings, but after recalling the effects of jubilation, one should not be quick to judge. Movements in Topeka, Kansas and in Los Angeles made headlines, and people started to wonder more and more about this gift of tongues. These movements so emphasized the importance of tongues that Catholics began to identify this gift as Protestant or non-Catholic.

However, there is evidence that Catholics may have preserved praying in tongues in the form of jubilation even in the 1930's and 40's. Ensely relates one story from Mr. Leonids Linauts, Professor of Stained Glass at Rochester Institute of Technology: "Mr. Linauts, a native of Latvia, and an expert on Latvia folklore, shed some light on the styles of prayer among the common people of this area. Before World War II when Mr. Linauts was a graduate student at the University of Riga, he spent his summers in the countryside collecting Latvia folklore. He said that it was the custom in some regions of Latvia, particularly the Aswege region, for parishioners to arrive an hour or so before Mass for singing and prayer. At times during this period before Mass the group would improvise wordless sounds and songs to express religious emotion."[142]

Vatican II to the Present

Pope John XXIII ushered in the Second Vatican Council with the hope that the Holy Spirit would create a "New Pentecost" and a transformation of the Church. His prayer to the Holy Spirit petitioned for the revival of the gifts given at Pentecost. This devotion to the Holy Spirit carried over into the Council.

In 1964, the fathers of the Second Vatican Council, in the

"Dogmatic Constitution on the Church," *Lumen Gentium*, state: "It is not only through the sacraments and the ministration of the Church that the Holy Spirit makes holy the People, leads them and enriches them with his virtues. Allotting his gifts according as he wills (cf. 1 Cor. 12:11), he also distributes special graces among the faithful of every rank. By these gifts he makes them fit and ready to undertake the various tasks or offices for the renewal and building up of the Church. ...Whether these charisms be very remarkable or more simple and widely diffused, they are fitting and useful for the needs of the Church."[143]

And in the "Decree on the Apostolate of the Laity," *Apostolicam Actuositatem*, the Vatican Council II fathers speak of the gift of the Holy Spirit and His charisms; making reference to the lists of charisms found in 1 Cor. 12:7-10, among which tongues is included: "From the reception of these charisms, even the most ordinary ones, there arises for each of the faithful the right and duty of exercising them in the Church and in the world for the good of men and the development of the Church, of exercising them in the freedom of the Holy Spirit who 'breathes where He wills.'"[144]

Pope Paul VI (1963-1978) also encouraged the exercise of the charisms and continually proclaimed the necessity of the Holy Spirit to manifest Christ's presence in the Church: "The Church needs her perennial Pentecost; she needs fire in the heart, words on the lips, prophecy in the glance. The Church needs to be the temple of the Holy Spirit."[145] And again: "The Church lives on the Holy Spirit. The Church was truly born, you could say, on the day of Pentecost. The Church's first need is always to live Pentecost."[146]

What is living Pentecost? It would appear that one be open to the reception of the Holy Spirit, accepting the various gifts offered and giving witness to Christ by prayer and edification of the Church. The prayer of Pope John XXIII was answered with the calling of the Second Vatican Council, and following the Council various confirmations of the presence of a "New Pentecost" began to emerge in the Catholic Church.

In 1966, four college professors at Duquesne University in Pittsburgh, Pennsylvania started to pray together in the hope of stirring up a new fervor in their Catholic faith. After a year of forming their group, reading scripture, praying, and asking for a new outpouring of the Holy Spirit, they received the "baptism in the Holy Spirit, and with this the gift of tongues."[147]

In February of 1967, the same faculty members and a small group of students from Duquesne went on a week-end retreat — about thirty persons in all.

This famous "Duquesne Week-end" as it has come to be called, was certainly one of the most remarkable incidents in the story of the Pentecostal movement. ...One engaged couple had heard about the "baptism in the Holy Spirit" and they desired it. So they approached the faculty members and asked them to pray with them that the Holy Spirit would become more fully active in their lives. Quietly they slipped upstairs, away from the crowd, and there, in prayer, they were deeply touched by the Spirit of Christ. The Spirit soon manifested himself in the gift of tongues with which the young man and woman praised God. ...What they did not know was that simultaneously one of the girls...had felt drawn to the chapel, and there had felt the almost tangible presence of the Spirit of Christ. In awe she left the chapel and quickly urged others in the building to join her there. By ones and twos the small group made their way to the chapel. And as they were gathered together there in prayer, the Holy Spirit poured himself out upon them.

There was no urging; there was no direction as to what had to be done. The individuals simply encountered the person of the Holy Spirit as others had several weeks before. Some praised God in new languages; others quietly wept for joy; others prayed and sang. They prayed from ten in the evening until five in the morning. Not everyone was touched immediately but throughout the evening God dealt with each person in a wonderful way.[148]

When the Catholic Charismatic Movement began in 1967, at Duquesne University, it appeared to have been part of the answer to the prayer of John XXIII and the encouragement of Paul VI. Since then this movement has spread all over the world. It has brought a tremendous resurgence of life in the body of Christ. The fruit of the movement has grown through many conversions to Christ, through a more profound understanding of discipleship, and through a deeper call to holiness. *The Malines Document*, written in 1974, believes that the Charismatic Renewal can be used in evangelization, catechesis, and the building up of the community.

"The renewal then makes the same request to the ecclesiastical authorities and to all concerned as that made by Popes John and Paul and repeatedly made at the Council, namely that all 'be open to what the Spirit is saying to the churches!' *Lumen Gentium* asked those who preside over the churches 'not to extinguish the Spirit, but to test all things and hold fast to that which is good' (n. 12; cf. 1 Thess. 5:12, 19-21).[149]

To some, this movement seemed to inaugurate a new, refreshing spirituality, but in reality it was a renewal of a very ancient expression of Christian prayer and practice. Although not the central focus, the charism of tongues was and still is integral to the Charismatic movement in the Catholic Church. It is the same gift of prayer that has moved Christians for centuries to a deeper union with God and has also provided edification in the Church. The Charismatic renewal, with all its holy fruit, has opened the door for people to see that the gift of tongues is not only a legitimate charism, but one given for common use to aid in the upbuilding of the people of God.

In reflecting on the mission on the Church, Pope John Paul II spoke at a general audience in September of 1989, about the tradition of Pentecost and how the descent of the Holy Spirit upon the apostles compelled them to go out and bring the presence of Christ to all. "Under the action of the Holy Spirit, the 'tongues of fire' became the word on the lips of the apostles: 'They were all filled with the Holy Spirit and began to speak in other tongues, as the Spirit gave them utterance.'"[150]

The Holy Father continues by commenting on the two different experiences of tongues which accompanied the descent of the Holy Spirit — the proclamation of the word of God and the praise of God in prayer:

> This happened in the Upper Room, but very soon the missionary proclamation and glossolalia, or gift of tongues, went beyond the place where they dwelt. Two extraordinary events took place, and they are described in the Acts of the Apostles. First of all, there is the gift of tongues by which they spoke words pertaining to a multiplicity of languages and used to sing the praises of God. ...The other extraordinary fact is the courage with which Peter and the Eleven "stood up" and began to explain the messianic and pneumatological meaning of what had happened before the eyes of that bewildered multitude. ...From Christ, to the apostles, to the Church, to the whole world: Under the action of the Holy Spirit the process of the universal unification in truth and love can and must unfold.[151]

The Pope sees the role of tongues as demonstrated in the apostles as an instrument of unity. This charism was important enough for the Holy Spirit to have used it to celebrate the birth of the Church, and empower individuals to go out and spread the good news of the resurrected Christ. Recognition should be given to the fact that the charism of tongues needs to be integrated with the other gifts of witnessing to Christ, and not be allowed to monopolize the area of proclaiming the good news.

The Holy Father states an appreciation for charisms in general, but also realizes the value of discernment and the proper use of charisms in ministry: "They are a singularly rich source of grace for the vitality of the apostolate and for the holiness of the whole Body of Christ, provided that they are gifts that come truly from the Spirit and are exercised in full conformity with the authentic promptings of the Spirit. In this sense the discernment of charisms is always necessary."[152]

The presence of the charism of tongues, as we have seen, has been a source of prayer and edification of the Church throughout the ages. Now that some of the past experience of this charism has been presented, a more detailed account of contemporary types and distinctions of the charism of tongues can also give a deeper understanding of this gift.

END NOTES PART II

[59] *The New Oxford Annotated Bible*, Revised Standard Edition, p. 1238.

[60] James Dunn, *Baptism in the Holy Spirit*, p. 41.

[61] Knofel Stanton, *Spiritual Gifts For Christians Today*, p. 63.

[62] Vincent Walsh, *A Key to the Charismatic Renewal*, p. 62.

[63] Dunn, *Baptism in the Holy Spirit*, p. 54.

[64] Ibid., p. 80.

[65] Ibid., p. 81.

[66] Ibid., p. 86.

[67] Ibid., p. 89.

[68] *L'encyclopedie des Musiques Sacres, vol.* II, pg. 26; translated by Ensely, E., *Sounds of Wonder*, p. 116.

[69] Francis Sullivan, S.J., *Charisms and Charismatic Renewal, p.* 22.

[70] Jerome Murphy-O'Connor, *The New Jerome Biblical Commentary*, p. 811.

[71] Ibid.

[72] William Richardson, *New Testament Studies*, vol. 32, "Liturgical Order and Glossolalia in I Corinthians 14:26c-33a," p. 147.

[73] C. K. Barret. *New International Commentary on the New Testament*, p. 317.

[74] Murphy O'Connor. p. 81.

[75] Scott Hahn, *New Pentecost*, "What's the Cost of Pentecost?", tape 2., 1992.

[76] B. C. Johanson. *New Testament Studies,* p. 193.

[77] Hahn.

[78] Ibid.

[79] *New American Bible*, Saint Joseph Edition, transliteration from the footnote, v. 28:9f, p. 850.

[80] Hahn.

[81] Ibid.

[82] Ibid.

[83] *New American Bible,* St. Joseph Edition, notes on 1 Cor. 14:20-22, p. 780.

[84] Hahn.

[85] Richardson. p. 149.

[86] Barret. p. 329.

[87] Ibid. p. 330.

[88] Kelsey, Morton, *Tongue Speaking*, p. 33.

[89] Ibid., pp. 34-35.

[90] Kelsey, *Tongue Speaking*, pp. 35-36.

[91] Ibid., pp. 36-37.

[92] René Laurentin, *Catholic Pentecostalism*, p. 155.

[93] Cecil A Roebeck, Jr., *Charismatic Experience in History,* "Origen's Treatment of the Charismata," p. 119.

[94] Ibid., Origen, *Homily on Exodus*, 13.2.

[95] Ibid., Origen, *On Prayer*, 2.4.

[96] Ibid.

[97] Ibid.

[98] Hampsch, *The Gift of Tongues*, Tape #2

[99] Ensely, *Sounds of Wonder*, p. 3.

[100] E. Ensely supplies an informative history of the charism of jubilation in his book, *Sounds of Wonder*.

[101] St. Augustine: "The Retractions," *The Fathers of the Church*, vol. 60, p. 55.

[102] Ensely, *Sounds of Wonder*, p. 40.

[103] Ibid., p. 40; St. Augustine, *Homilies on the First Epistle of John, Nicene and Post-Nicene Fathers, VI*, p. 10.

[104] Ibid., pg. 40; St. Augustine, *On Baptism, Against the Donatists, III, XVIII*, 16.21.

[105] Ibid., p. 8; St. Augustine, *Commentary on the Psalms, "Ennar. in Ps. 97, 4,"* PL 37, pp. 1254-5, translated by Abbot David Geraets, O.S.B.

[106] Ibid., p. 8.

[107] Ensely, *Sounds of Wonder*, p. 20.

[108] Ibid., p. 7.

[109] Ibid., p. 9.

[110] Ibid., p. 10; Marcus Aureli Cassidori, *Exposition in Psalterium Ps. 65, 1, in PL 70*, p. 451.

[111] Ensely, *Sounds of Wonder*, p. 11; Isidore of Seville, Opera Omnia, V. 43.

[112] Ibid., pp. 32-46.

[113] Ibid., p. 50.

[114] Ensely, *Sounds of Wonder*, p. 80.

[115] Ibid., p. 4; Thomas Aquinas, *Psalterium David, in Ps. 32, 3.*

[116] Ibid., p. 54-55.

[117] Ibid., p. 82-83; John Ruysbroeck, *The Kingdom of Lovers of God*, translated by T. Arnold Hyde, p.89.

[118] Ensely, *Sounds of Wonder*, p. 84; John G. Artinero, *Mystical Evolution in the Development and Vitality of the Church,* vol.II, p. 76.

[119] Ibid., p. 87; Richard Rolle, *Contra Amores Mundi*, p. 26.

[120] Ibid., p. 68.

[121] Hampsch, *The Gifts of Tongues*, Tape #2.

[122] Charles Warren Stoddard, *Saint Anthony, The Wonder-Worker of Padua*, p.41.

[123] Hampsch, *The Gifts of Tongues*, Tape #2.

[124] Kelsey, *Tongue Speaking*, p. 50.

[125] Aquinas, *Summa Theologiae,* II, q. 176 a. 1.

[126] Ibid., a. 2.

[127] Ibid.

[128] Ibid.

[129] DeGrandis, *The Gift of Miracles*, p. 27.

[130] Ensely, *Sounds Of Wonder*, pp. 75, 76.

[131] Ibid., pp. 90-95.

[132] Ibid., p. 94; St. Teresa of Avila, *Interior Castles*, translated and edited by E. Allison Peers, p. 169.

[133] Ibid., p. 169.

[134] Ensely, *Sounds of Wonder,* p. 95; *St. Teresa of Avila,* Autobiography of Teresa of Avila, translated and edited by E. Allison Peers, pp. 164-5.

[135] Ibid., pp. 96, 97, 103.

[136] Kelsey, *Tongue Speaking,* p. 49.

[137] Ibid., p. 55.

[138] Ibid., pp. 52-54.

[139] Simon Tugwell, *Have You Received the Spirit?,* p. 67.

[140] H.I. Lederle, *Treasures Old and New,* pg. 5. For a more thorough study on this, H.I. Lederle's *Treasures Old and New* gives good background on various theologies on Spirit-baptism.

[141] Tugwell, *Have You Received the Spirit?,* p. 67.

[142] Ensely, *Sounds of Wonder,* p. 109.

[143] *Lumen Gentium,* no. 12.

[144] *Apostolicam Actuositatem,* no. 3.

[145] Pope Paul VI, *Address to the General Audience, Nov. 29, 1972* (translated from *L' Osservatore Romano,* English language edition, Dec. 7, 1972, 1).

[146] Ibid., "The Holy Spirit and the Life of the Church," *Address to the General Audience, Oct. 12, 1966;* translation from *The Pope Speaks, 12:1, (1967)* 79-81.

[147] Ranaghan, *Catholic Pentecostals Today,* p. 17.

[148] Ibid., p. 20.

[149] *Theological and Pastoral Orientations on the Catholic Charismatic Renewal,* p. 52.

[150] Pope John Paul II, "The Beginning of the Church's Mission," *General Audience, September 20, 1989.* Translation from *The Pope Speaks,* vol. 35:1 (1990), 38.

[151] Ibid.

[152] Pope John Paul II, *Christifideles Laici,* p. 60.

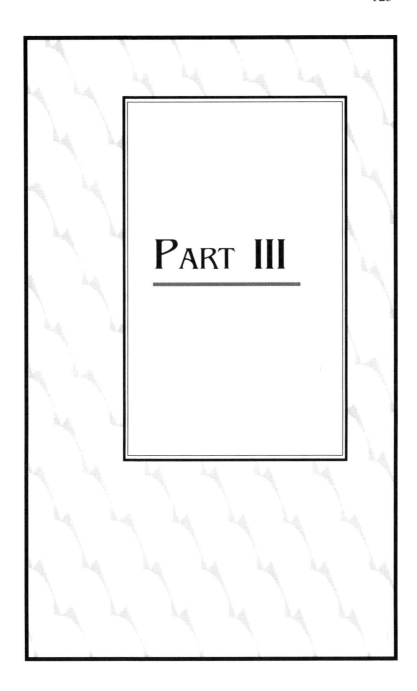

PART III

PART III

THE TYPOLOGY OF THE CHARISM OF TONGUES

The New Testament records three expressions of the charisms of tongues: praying in tongues, singing in tongues (the direction is from us to God) and speaking in tongues (prophetic tongues), which works together with the charism of interpretation of tongues (1 Cor. 14:2; the direction is from God to us). Within the expression of praying in tongues, John Hampsch, C.M.F. identifies four levels.[153]

Praying in Tongues

1. The Pre-linguistic Level of Tongues

This stage of tongues is most evident when people first open themselves to the Spirit and begin to use the gift. It is glossolalia-like, because the sounds are unintelligible; sometimes very similar to the sound of a hum or a whistle. Although the sounds do not articulate syllables, it is nevertheless real prayer because the intention to pray is operative. On occasion, the Holy Spirit instantly, gives someone the gift of an advanced "prayer language" in tongues — either glossolalia or xenolalia — but most people experience a gradual growth in this charism of prayer.

At this pre-linguistic level, there is usually no pronunciation of words. An individual's beginning prayer may also be just a fluttering of the tongue or a sounding of vowel sounds, but it is still prayer. Sometimes this is similar to a type of jubilation where only vowel sounds are sung or prayed. Some people find it difficult to move beyond this initial stage and can even lose their desire to use the gift. This is because praying in tongues does not need to be dramatic. So, if our expectation is for something sensational, we might have the tendency to believe that nothing explicit is really happening or that we are not being edified personally.[154] This is the novice level of tongues, and we need to realize this. A gift can only grow and mature if it is exercised. Artists improve on their talent by painting, athletes by putting forth an effort in their sport, and so it is the same with charismatic gifts. They become stronger and more operative in a person when they are used frequently. [155]

Tongues, along with the other word gifts, can only happen if I open my mouth and use my voice to utter syllables which can be heard. God does not usually take control of a person's tongue in such a way that one *automatically* starts praying in tongues. Yielding to the gift of tongues by asking the Holy Spirit to bestow the charism will open the person to manifest tongues. Then the prayerful sounds will eventually become a more articulate form of the gift.

2. The Linguistic Level of Tongues

If the gift of prayer tongues is used, eventually there will be noticeable changes, including inflection, diction, fluency, and articulation.[156] These are the signs and characteristics of a developing language; the recipient is now ready to move on to the linguistic level. This does not necessarily imply that the prayer in tongues turns into an actual language, but rather that the glossolalia has language-like characteristics. At this level xenolalia can also occur. Fr. Hampsch claims, "The change of tongues can be one of the 5000 living languages, from the some 10,000 dead languages, a future language, or an unearthly language like the tongues of angels, or God can give you your own prayer language."[157] There is no way of knowing for sure what "language" a person is using unless another person knows the language being spoken in prayer — and this is not routine. If there is a noticeable change in tongues in pronunciation and fluency, then more than likely the person is at the linguistic level. Fr. Hampsch gives simple advice about developing tongues in the linguistic mode of tongues:

> Let yourself develop syllables, but try not to be redundant. As soon as you notice redundancy, try to change the articulation and sound of the words, and keep doing this until there is no or minimal repetition. Let articulation flow. There is one type of utterance that can develop into a language, and another that will not because it is simply a fluttering of the tongue. Leaders need to aid people to move deeper into the gift of praying in tongues. Articulate, it is not artificial....If there is any thing artificial about tongues it will not last long, only momentarily. It takes humility, like a baby. It seems foolish, but pride keeps us from praying in tongues. Once you get over the hump of pride, tongues develop.[158]

3. Jubilation in Tongues

As mentioned before, jubilation can be expressed in

several ways; only one of which is tongues. Tongues of jubilation are tongues of rejoicing. When a person has predisposed oneself to praise in a spirit of joy, it is a manifestation of a deeper union with God. This gives a profound sense of release to the individual to let the jubilation tongues freely flow out as the Spirit prompts. When this happens the Spirit is operating at a higher level of praise. Jubilation tongues can be manifested through singing or vocal prayer either privately or in unison with a congregation.

Ensley discusses a third manifestation of jubilation tongues which he calls *mystical jubilation.* Pope St. Gregory the Great described this type of jubilation as coming from the heart with such great joy that words are useless, "yet despite this, the heart vents what it is feeling by means of the voice; what it cannot express by discursive speech."[159] John Joseph Gorre is an early nineteenth century author who wrote about mystical jubilation. In his work *Die Christliche Mystik,* Gorre devotes an entire chapter to jubilation which he titles "The Effect of Ecstasy on the Organs of the Voice."[160] He describes the use of normal speech patterns that change as the ecstasy unfolds. "The forces which contribute to the formation of this sound (ordinary speech) can also submit to a transformation in ecstasy and the sounds produced in this state carry a character which is much different from ordinary sounds....The spirit itself is articulated in these sounds — words which the spirit of man hadn't thought. The voice then produces sounds which seem to belong to someone else. Or if this is really the voice of one speaking, it is like elevated or winged thoughts which are spoken."[161]

Mystical jubilation leads the person into higher levels of contemplative prayer. The more contemplative the tongues, the more the Holy Spirit draws the person deeper into union with God, which can lead to the final stage of prayer tongues, ecstatic utterance.

4. Ecstatic utterance

Ecstatic utterances is a high form of jubilation tongues that brings a person into infused contemplation. When people refer to "tongues" they usually mean basic prayer tongues; the person is not in an ecstatic state. Ecstatic utterance, however, refers to a more advanced experience of this charism of prayer which disposes one to infused contemplation. The Spirit can move the person into contemplation and inspire him or her to jubilate in tongues, or the tongues may be used as an instrument to move the person into contemplation.

> The first recorded use was by the Hesecastic fathers, who were semi-hermits in the deserts of the Middle East. And this was practiced by the monks at Mt. Athos up until the fourteenth century. They began this by praising God in "a language not their own," and it developed into a refined prayer form. They would gather or walk in small groups of two or three and praising God. They would then enter into a very high level of deep contemplative praise and go into ecstasy. They were then unable to speak and fell into a profound silence. The fourth level of tongues crescendos into such high praise that they could not speak anymore and entered into infused contemplative prayer.[162]

Teresa of Avila may have referred to this when she described certain responses to "be unutterable utterances" when the Spirit moved her into contemplation.[163] Teresa's description is related to an ecstatic experience in the Spirit, and the jubilation tongues she describes seems to be the response rather than the cause of the ecstasy. This would appear to be the elevated level of prayer tongues. Hampsch believes, "One of the fastest ways of becoming a mystic, in the traditional Catholic sense, is to develop the fourth level of tongues. This is how precious this beautiful gift of tongues is."[164]

Singing in Tongues

When we exercise singing in tongues (1 Cor. 14:15) the direction is usually from us to God. St. Paul tells us to sing songs in the Spirit and harmonize in the Spirit (Col. 3:14-16; Eph. 4:3, 5:19). This expression of the charism of tongues has the same four levels or modes as praying in tongues, but it has the added dimension of music. When a person, small group, or whole congregation is open to the movement of the Spirit in the singing in tongues, the elements of the music can sometimes be miraculous. Professional musicians and composers who do not know about tongues are often amazed at the harmonies that are reached from untrained singers. After a large gathering at a Loyola Marymount University (Los Angeles) prayer meeting a professional musician stated in amazement:

> These people are singing the seventh dominate chord with perfect counterpoint and harmony. You could not do this with a 100 person choir without many, many hours of practice with an expert director, and people who really know what they are doing to blend those chords.

And here all of these things are happening without any practice, without leadership. Just people singing and the seventh dominate chord is coming out. This is absolutely incredible. That is a miracle to me as a musician.[165]

On the power of tongues in music, a religious sister who was present at the Notre Dame Charismatic Conference in 1967 said: "In regard to the 'unknown tongues' a musically trained mind and ear, accustomed to hearing rhythms and nuances, accustomed to analyzing tonal patterns, and balances, unconsciously seeks and discerns structures of audible forms. The identifying parallels between patterns of sound in the tongues and those in interpretation or translation which invariably followed when tongues were spoken in the assembly were sometimes quite apparent…At the same time the prayers uttered in this manner were gems of poetic composition and content — too much so to have been composed on the spur of the moment by amateurs."[166]

The gift of singing in tongues can also be used to measure the degree of unity in a particular group or assembly. If anyone is harboring resentment, bitterness or hatred in the heart, it seems to produce a manifestation of disharmony in a group when singing in tongues.[167] Jesus said to reconcile with your brother or sister before you worship, so you can offer a pure prayer. When persons are not reconciled, their prayer power is diminished. With tongues the power of the prayer seems to be more distinguishable. The resulting harmony can be a tremendous gift from God as a sign of unity and love.

Speaking in Tongues

In this expression of tongues the direction is from God to us (1 Cor. 14:5-2). Speaking in tongues is also known as prophetic tongues or authoritative tongues because it must be coupled with interpretation. In this instance, tongues is connected with prophecy. In Acts 2:14-18, Peter identifies tongues with prophecy. Paul, on the other hand, distinguishes tongues from prophecy, but equates the two when the charism of interpretation is used.[168]

Prophecy is the greatest of the spiritual charisms (1 Cor. 14:1), and one of its forms is in tongues with interpretation of tongues. Hampsch gives us his explanation of prophetic tongues: "God takes a prophecy and reinforces it by surrounding it in three minor miracles: One speaks a prophecy in a language they do not know, then someone else or the same person interprets or translates from a language they do not know, and thirdly there is the powerful impact of the inspiration. The Holy Spirit presents a message from God and enhances it to give a strongly impacted prophecy to the community, more often than not, in response to the singing or praying in tongues as a community."[169]

This type of tongues can be either glossolalic or xenolalic in nature. The exercise of this gift is commonly experienced within prayer groups by those who also exercise the gift of praying in tongues. The sequence usually begins when the people involved begin to sing or pray in tongues for a short period of time followed by a period of silence. If someone receives a prophecy, it is usually given at this time; including speaking in tongues. This situation seems to be similar to that which Paul was writing about in 1 Cor. 14. A prophecy in tongues needs to be interpreted into the vernacular or the native language of the people to edify the community. After the person is finished speaking in tongues, there is a brief period of silence while the community waits for the Spirit to give the interpretation, which is spoken in the vernacular. Sometimes the same person who has spoken in tongues is also given the gift of interpretation; at other times the interpretation comes from another. DeGrandis calls this a "charismatic cycle." The community speaks to God through tongues of praise, thanksgiving, and petition in the Spirit, and then God responds in the Spirit by giving a prophecy, either in tongues or in the language of the people.[170]

Paul says this type of tongues is a sign for the *apistoi* (the unsaved or unbeliever or someone ignorant of spiritual gifts), but only when accompanied by interpretation (1 Cor. 14:22-25); only then does it take on the strength of prophecy. It can only help these people if the meaning of what was uttered in the Spirit is given to them in an understandable manner. The gifts of tongues and interpretation can edify the people present, believers and unbelievers alike, because these are powerful instruments that can expose people to an external experience of God, and thus open them more completely to deeper internal encounters with the Spirit of Christ.

Speaking in tongues can be a gift for preaching and

evangelization, as was shown by the famous example of St. Vincent Ferrer. This happens not only when a person is engaged in preaching, but more commonly when someone is praying or singing. The person may be in a mode of praying or singing, but then the Spirit uses the tongues as prophecy in a xenolalic manner. In other words, a person may be praising God in tongues, but one or others will hear the words in their own language. Thus, the person praying in tongues has no knowledge of praying in a known language. At Pentecost, there were similar effects when the apostles were praying in tongues; the people heard them in their own language. This miraculous gift of God's power leads an unbeliever to become a Christian. Today, it is not as common, but it still happens. Hampsch relates one story of a Japanese Buddhist:

> She went to a charismatic prayer meeting at the insistence of her American husband who was a Christian. A woman sitting in front of the couple was praying in tongues. The Japanese woman touched her shoulder when she had finished and said, 'I am impressed that you know my language, you were praying in perfect Japanese, but I am more curious how you know my secret temple name that is only known to me and only a few in Japan.' The woman who was praying in tongues was amazed that she was praying in Japanese. The Buddhist woman then said, 'I heard you say my secret temple name and then you said, 'You have searched for the truth all your life, now come to the fullness of truth. Come to me, I am Jesus Christ.' The Japanese woman received Baptism shortly after this experience.[171]

The Holy Spirit is often subtle about the manifestation of His spiritual gifts. His anointing can come upon one person distinctly different from another. DeGrandis gives an experience that provides a good example of this:

A woman stood up during a prayer meeting and spoke in tongues. A few minutes later another woman gave the interpretation of the prophetic tongues. Then a man spoke up and said, 'The first woman who spoke gave a beautiful message about the love of God. It touched my heart.' Then the other lady gave a paraphrase of that message. The man had *heard* the woman speaking in tongues in English, while everyone else heard only *foreign* tongues. Even the person who interpreted only received a paraphrase; she did not hear in English.[172]

The gifts of speaking in tongues with interpretation can also operate outside the context of prayer or prophecy. A person can receive the gift of speaking and understanding a language that was previously unknown, or the gift of understanding the language without being able to speak it. St. Vincent Ferrer is an example, but there have also been accounts of this happening in our era. Venerable Padre Pio (1887-1968), an Italian, Capuchin, stigmatist priest who received many mystical experiences and gifts, was said to have had this gift. And, Marija Pavlovic, one of the alleged visionaries of Medjugorje, is now fluent in Italian where previously she had no knowledge of it. She claims that after praying for the gift, she woke up one morning and was able to speak and understand the language. Fr. Luke Zimmer, SS.CC., founder of the Apostolate of Christian Renewal in California, can understand spoken Italian and Spanish perfectly but cannot speak either language himself. Because he has no prior knowledge of these languages we can say it is the manifestation of a gift of the Holy Spirit.[173]

Other Experiences of Speaking in Tongues

"Dialoguing in tongues," has only recently been discussed. This experience occurs when two people have a conversation in tongues; first one speaks, then the other. Although this phenomenon has not been solidly discerned, it appears simply to be prophetic tongues given by and for the two individuals. DeGrandis believes that the persons involved receive a sense of some work of grace being done; usually there is spiritual or emotional healing going on during the dialogue.[174]

Interpretation of tongues and prophecy are connected to this use of tongues. This unique use of the charism of tongues provides a building up of the persons involved. However, unless a person has experienced this particular gift there will not be sound teaching on it.

A religious sister who received baptism in the Spirit and the charism of tongues began using tongues in her ministry. One time she was asked by the father of one of her students to pray for him. She began to pray in tongues. The man interrupted the sister's prayer, asking her how she knew his native language. She said that she did not know his language and asked what it was. The man was Arabic. He was astounded and asked her to continue. He offered to translate for her. She spoke in Arabic and the man translated each phrase into English. Meanwhile another sister overheard what was going on and brought a tape recorder to capture the experience on tape. Afterwards, the man wrote in Arabic on the blackboard what had been said in tongues. It was a prayer of praise to God. The man had a deep conversion experience, and this gave his faith in Christ the powerful boost he needed. The next day the grandmother of another Arabic student of the school read the message on the blackboard and started to sing it. She said it was an Arabic hymn of praise to God that she used to sing when she was a young girl. It was based on one of the Psalms of praise in scripture.[175]

Again, these uses of the charism of tongues either edify the individual or others, as an experience of prayer, prophecy or preaching. Some are very common and others rare, but they are given to build up the Church, the body of Christ.

Tongues as a Charism of Private Prayer

A charism is given for the edification of the Church, but tongues seems to have the unique attribute of aiding in the person's own edification as well. Because the charism of tongues edifies the individual directly (uttering mysteries in the Spirit to God, 1 Cor. 14:2), it does not directly build up the community as powerfully as preaching, prophecy, miracles or other charisms. The edification it brings is most commonly practiced as a gift of prayer.

Francis Sullivan S.J. says, "I believe that when speaking [praying] in tongues is a genuine gift of grace, a 'charism,' it will prove to be a new gift of prayer, especially for the prayer of praise. The question whether speaking in tongues in any particular case is a genuine charism or not can be answered by asking what it does for a person's life of prayer."[176]

Fundamentally, the charism of tongues is a gift of prayer. It was given this way to the apostles at Pentecost; the other effects from the praise in tongues happened precisely because the Apostles were praying. Many people who have engaged in the practice of praying in tongues have said that their experience of prayer has improved positively and they have experienced a more profound presence of God in their lives. Praying in tongues can enhance and deepen our prayer life, and when our prayer life is enhanced, so is our quality of life in general. As Malcom Cornwell, C.P. comments, "Tongues edifies the person even though there is no understanding of what is being said. The word 'edify' may sound rather pious; what is meant is the constructive building of the tongue-speaker's personality."[177]

As mentioned previously, the gift of prayer tongues usually occurs when a person enters into higher levels of prayer. The Holy Spirit seems to bestow this gift to aid in "opening" a person to receive a more profound encounter with God. Wherever we are in the spiritual life, whether just beginning or already immersed in high degrees of contemplation, prayer tongues will be a catalyst to deepening prayer. However, as DeGrandis points out, to describe what happens in the interior of the human spirit can only be speculation.

The intimate details of tongues I cannot explain to you and I doubt that anyone could. Many conjecture, but to reveal intrinsically what it is, no one can. Neither can I intrinsically tell you what happens when I take the bread and wine during Mass and say, "This is my Body. This is My Blood." Theologically, I can speculate, but I can't tell you intrinsically what happens. It does happen and I know that by faith. I'll help you to yield to tongues and afterwards you can speculate yourself. The important thing is to have the experience yourself.[178]

What are the Advantages of Praying in Tongues?

New prayer power! This happens because the spirit of the person is inspired by the Holy Spirit to pray outside the realm of the mind.[179] As Paul relates, the Spirit teaches us how to pray; therefore, prayer tongues can be expressed as the Holy Spirit praying in my spirit. There is a surge of power because it is not the person praying, but the Holy Spirit praying (Rm. 8:21). Most often this spiritual prayer power leads to a strengthening of confidence in other forms of prayer, including silent prayer.

Another advantage of praying tongues is that this gift provides a new kind of freedom. Since this is a form of non-discursive prayer (the intellect is not involved), a person can use prayer tongues as a way of praying free from any mental distractions.[180]

This can be extremely helpful when a person is experiencing many distractions or dryness in prayer. Prayer tongues can be a healthy outlet to aid in moving through this period.

A third advantage could be in the area of intercessory

prayer. Many times people find themselves not knowing what to pray for or how to pray in a given situation. Tongues can be an effective means of intercession. Again, since the Holy Spirit is praying within us, the Spirit knows what to pray for better than we do. Hampsch agrees with this notion:

> …And the Spirit will pray in you. The spirit of the person stays in a spontaneous mode which allows the Holy Spirit to flow more freely. You do not have to worry about what to say and gives you a whole new freedom, and language [a prayer language] is still being used. My spirit is encountering God's spirit in prayer. My mind is not in it. This charism becomes a vehicle of praise, and the Spirit of God using the faculties of mind and speech, putting them together in marvelous blending and coordination ascending as a beautiful prayer to God, and transcendentalizing or sublimating your highest faculties, your mind and speech faculty. [181]

Praying in tongues also helps the person fulfill Christ's command to pray always; it is a doorway to charismatic ministries because the use of prayer tongues somehow sensitizes the person to yield to other charismatic activities of the Holy Spirit. It is a personal, concrete sign of God's action within, and it is a powerful weapon against Satan. [182]

Tongues as Contemplation

Robert Faricy, S.J., a professor of theology at the Gregorian University in Rome, believes prayer tongues to be an authentic vehicle of contemplative prayer. "The gift of tongues is, itself, a gift of contemplative prayer. To receive the gift of tongues is to receive a gift of contemplation." [183] Faricy is also involved in the Charismatic Renewal and conducts seminars and workshops to help people yield to the tongues.

> When I pray in tongues, I babble; linguistically, I am saying or singing gibberish. The meaning is not in the sounds, as though they were words that represented concepts. The meaning of prayer in tongues lies in the heart because prayer tongues is non-conceptual. The sounds are not words; they have no conceptual meaning. They are just meaningless syllables. Praying in tongues is vocalized non-conceptual prayer. It is noisy contemplation.[184]

The Malines Document also describes prayer tongues in a similar way, and says that the one who prays in tongues usually has alternative ways of praying:

> If persons esteem this charism, it is because they want to pray better, and the charism of tongues helps them to do just that. Its principal function is to be found in private prayer. There is considerable spiritual value in having a pre-conceptual nonobjective way of praying. It allows one to say in a different, pre-conceptual medium what could not be said in a conceptual medium. Praying in tongues is to prayer what an abstract, nonobjective picture is to painting. Praying in tongues requires intelligence, discipline, and form, of which even children are capable. Under the power of the Spirit, the believer prays freely without conceptual forms. For people who pray in tongues this is only one of a number of forms of prayer.[185]

Praying in Tongues with the Community

Praying or singing in tongues with others has proven to be an experience that provides positive spiritual fruit. Praying in this way as a community is another way to unite the voices of the Body of Christ to communicate gifts of praise to God; it is representative of one People of God. Where two or three are gathered in the name of Jesus, He is there; made present by the power of the Holy Spirit. Community tongue praying can be an edifying experience both personally and for the assembly. As was mentioned earlier, it opens many avenues of prayer and allows the Lord to speak to the community through the word gifts of wisdom, knowledge, and prophecy. DeGrandis believes that tongues and prophecy are the skeleton of this type of community prayer:

> Why such an emphasis on tongues? Prayer meetings are a dialogue of a community with the Lord. This is the value of it. The community goes to the Father in the Spirit; dubbed the 'charismatic cycle.' We go to the Father in tongues and he comes back to us in prophecy in Jesus' name, in the Spirit. Love is total communication, God is Love, God is communication. Tongues is spiritual communication from us to the Lord."[186]

The edification that flows from the tongues is from the prayer of praise. Praise of God from the heart always lifts the spirit, and this opens the window of the soul to God. God can begin to fill the person with graces, blessings and gifts which enable the person to continue to grow in his or her relationship with God. The charism of prayer tongues is an instrument of this encounter with God.

Pastoral Uses of the Charism of Tongues

Tongues as a gift for ministry seems contradictory to Paul's instructions about self-edification, but there is a special place for the charism of tongues in ministry. The main contribution of the Charismatic Renewal is the practice and promotion of the spiritual gifts listed in 1 Cor. 12:8-10. Paul, in his analogy of the Church as a human body, shows that the Body of Christ operates as one but with different gifts; here he gives another listing of charisms or persons who exercise certain charisms (1 Cor. 12:27-31). Some charismatic theologians, like Hampsch and DeGrandis, believe this listing is that of ministerial charisms, precisely because persons are named, not the gifts alone. In other words, being apostle, prophet, teacher, worker of miracles, healer, or speaker in tongues seems to be a list of persons who exercise these charisms, or who have been given these types of charismatic ministries.

Not all have these gifts, as Paul states. The one who speaks in tongues in this case is grouped with other gifts that seemed to be described as happening regularly in the person who has been given these charisms. Again, tongues is listed last for a reason. Paul wants to demonstrate to the Corinthians that tongues is not as great as the other charisms listed, even for those who are particularly strong in this charism. Even though Paul states that not all speak in tongues, later in 1 Cor. 14:5 his desire is for all to speak in tongues. Granted, wishing and stating a fact are two different things, but Paul could be bruising the ego of the tongue speakers who think their charismatic ministry is higher than that of the prophet or apostle; yet at the same time he wants to encourage people to use the charism of tongues. Whether this was Paul's intention or not, the charism of tongues, as a gift of prayer and of edification of the People of God, can be very beneficial in pastoral ministry, as has been shown throughout the history of the Church.

Tongues as a Ministry of Intercession

The spiritual gifts (1 Cor. 12:8-10) are the "tools of the trade" for ministry, whether in preaching, teaching, healing, or intercessory prayer. Since the charism of tongues is a gift of prayer, it can be used as an *instrument of intercession.* Because tongues is a "free-floating" gift; not an institutionalized charism, it is, in a sense, a ministry within ministries. Thus, the charism can be an instrument used *in* ministry, but not as *a* ministry.

This prayer of intercession in tongues can certainly be exercised privately by anyone who has special intentions, but the emphasis here is on public ministry practiced by one person or a group of people. Using prayer tongues regularly and having a particular strength in this area can be a good indication that the person may be called to exercise prayer tongues as a tool for intercession.[187]

Discernment and common sense is also applied here, because sometimes the person or persons being prayed for may not be aware of what tongues is, and may be distracted or even frightened by it. Proper explanation should be given to help people understand what is happening.

Tongues in the Ministry of Healing and Miracles

Whenever Jesus sent the twelve apostles and the seventy-two disciples to preach the gospel, he also told them to heal the sick. (Matt. 10:7-8; Mk. 6:12-13; 16:16-20; Luke 10:8-9). As Christians, we are also called by Christ to do the same. This can happen at least by proclaiming the gospel through the daily living of Christ's message and by bringing healing through our private prayer and reconciliation with others. The two charisms of healing and miracles are obvious signs of God's power, and they are given to build up the virtues of faith, hope and love.

Healing and miracles are gifts that everyone can participate in, and they are positive answers to prayer. Experience indicates that sooner or later, if I believe and pray, I will be involved with some type of healing or a miracle. The charism of tongues, since it is fundamentally a gift of prayer, can be a catalyst for the manifestation of healings and miracles. In an atmosphere of praising God in tongues we may become more predisposed and thus a healing may be received more readily.

DeGrandis, Hampsch, and others whom God uses in the ministry of healing and miracles say that tongues is necessary in their ministry because through praying in tongues the other gifts (word of wisdom and knowledge, discernment, faith, healing, miracles, prophecy, interpretation of tongues) are activated. It seems then, that when one prays in tongues for a particular healing, or even a miracle, the use of this gift helps one become a more open conduit for the grace of God to operate.

Cardinal Suenens also believes that praying in tongues can even provide an environment where healing occurs for ourselves: "This prayer within the depths of our being, heals at a profound yet often imperceptible level, the hidden psychological wounds that impede the full development of our interior life."[188]

DeGrandis oftentimes asks people who need emotional or inner healing to start praying in tongues because he believes "...tongues begins the cleaning purification process in the unconscious. [Tongues as] holistic prayer edifies the mind, body, and spirit; brings the emotions that are buried in subconscious to a conscious level. There is a lot of self-healing in praying in tongues."[189]

It is important for us to know that one of the continuous ministries in the Church is healing. It is given through the sacraments, the sacramentals *and* the spiritual charisms. When the charism of tongues is used in the healing ministry it can be another avenue that God uses in working miracles for His people.

Tongues as an Instrument in Exorcism

Here the term *exorcism* is used in a more general way and not as a deliverance from diabolical possession where the permission of the diocesan bishop is required. This general usage refers more to what is sometimes called a simple deliverance or minor exorcism from evil or evil habits. This is a healing on the spiritual level, and the same principle that was given for healing with regard to tongues can be applied in this area.

"The exercise of all the charismatic gifts is essentially a ministry of love, edification, upbuilding and deliverance," as Kevin and Dorothy Ranaghan state.[190] It appears to be evident that in the charism of tongues, the Lord is giving us the necessary prayer to offer on behalf of oneself or another. Just as Jesus is the Baptizer in the Spirit, so he is the Deliverer, and the Savior.

There is a particular power over evil when praying in tongues, simply because it is praise of God. Praise was rejected by the devil and his angels, and now that Christ has rescued humanity from the power of Satan, the praise of God can act like "a two edged-sword to deal out vengeance" to the enemies of God (Ps. 149). DeGrandis points to praise as the very power that tongues has over evil.

In the area of "spiritual warfare," DeGrandis notes that in his experience, tongues is essential for this type of healing ministry. He also warns that people should not get involved in this area of ministry unless they have knowledge, experience and are spiritually equipped to minister in this realm. Someone who does not know what he or she is doing can create a worse situation.[191]

Fr. DeGrandis comments about what happens when someone begins to pray in tongues for an individual who needs
deliverance. The sounds of the prayer language will usually
change in intonation and become more *war-like*. "Tongues
change with emotions and in a change in spiritual levels; also
doing a deliverance can change tongues. They can become
more bellicose."[192] He also has experienced many people who
have received healings from addictions, from emotional and
spiritual problems, and even from physical disabilities by
praying in tongues as a means of deliverance from evil.

Tongues Can Help Others Yield to the Spirit

Basically, this comes back full circle to the original
premise that the charism of tongues is a gift of prayer and
edification for the Church. Pastors, church leaders, lay and
religious can use this gift of prayer to help others experience
God. DeGrandis, speaking at a workshop on spiritual gifts in
1986, made an alarming statement: "I personally believe that
because the charismatic gifts are not accepted within the
Church and not common, that Christianity is in a decaying
condition. We have an anemic Christianity because the gifts
of the Spirit are not active within the Church."[193]

Unfortunately, having an *experience* of God is lacking in
many parishes. This situation is probably due to passivity and
a lack of knowledge about faith. People desire an authentic
experience of the Spirit of God. The gift of tongues can ini-

tiate an encounter with the Lord that is simple yet profound. This is true mainly because tongues is an obvious manifestation of the Holy Spirit.

When I was working at a Catholic leadership training camp for thirteen and fourteen year olds, I experienced an event that confirms this. One evening I was asked to lead a time of prayer in the girls' cabin. An adult leader, who knows that I am involved in the Charismatic Renewal, asked me not to do anything "charismatic." I assured the person that nothing would be initiated.

When I arrived at the cabin I was surprised to find twenty-five girls and their adult leaders waiting for me. What I thought was going to be a quiet time of prayer turned out to be a question and answer session. One of the girls asked, "Father Mike, what is the gift of tongues?" Since I did not initiate the conversation, I figured I was safe to finish it. I proceeded to explain this gift and its purpose. Then I said, "I think everyone would have a better understanding of the gift of tongues if you experienced it."

All of the girls and their leaders were open to the experience. I assured them that one person is not better than another if some acquire the gift and other do not. But I did say that, "The Holy Spirit will not give this gift if you do not yield your voice to the Spirit." They all nodded their heads, and then I led them in singing a chorus of the eight-fold Alleluia. Immediately afterward, all but one or two were singing in tongues for the first time. It was one of the most beautiful harmonies I have ever heard.

We then repeated the "Alleluia" and the other girls began to open their mouths and chime in with the group. About half of the group experienced other manifestations of the Holy Spirit: For some, warmth was flowing into their hands, over their heads and shoulders; others just experienced a profound peace and sense of safety. Many shared how they felt that Jesus was very close to them. Almost all of these teenage girls had a sense of joy and knew that God loved them. Two girls approached me the next day and told me that they stayed up late that night and prayed together in tongues. They also shared how they experienced a calling to pray more in their daily lives.

As has been shown many times, the spiritual charisms are a channel for an initial encounter with the Holy Spirit that can only broaden and deepen our relationship with Christ and the Church.

In 1974, after Vatican II, in his book *A New Pentecost?* Cardinal Suenens explains (in his section on tongues) how the charismatic dimension of tongues can activate renewal in individuals and thus become one way to effect a renewal in the Church; moving the Church beyond being inactive and lethargic as a community of faith:

> Let us admit it: We are terribly complicated when it comes to giving outward expression to our deep religious feelings before God or in front of others. Even priests and religious know at what cost they reveal themselves at any spiritual depth to those with whom they live, and how often community life is little more than superficial

juxtaposition of individual lives. We have been ossified by formalism
and ritualism. Our liturgical gatherings have only begun to awaken
to the meaning of communal liturgy after centuries of passivity. But
though a thaw has set in, we have yet to experience the warmth and
enthusiasm that should characterize our liturgical celebrations in
community.[194]

All over the world, people who have entered the Charismatic Movement have experienced these spiritual gifts and
have found that their relationship with the Lord and his Church
has been strengthened and become profoundly rich.
DeGrandis believes, "Once you go through the door of
tongues, you can go through the door of anything. One of the
most difficult things, I believe the average person can do, is
to yield their voice to the Lord in the gift of tongues. Once
you have, everything also becomes easier because this is one
of the foolish things you can do."[195]

Tongues has been a starting point for many who wanted
to deepen and expand their horizons of prayer. These testi-
monies from *The Gift of Tongues* by DeGrandis may be of
interest:

Myrtis

I had only been in the "Renewal" for one month when I received the
baptism in the Spirit and also the gift of tongues at the same time. I
was searching and I guess I was open because I had no problem
coming into the gift of tongues at the baptism of the Spirit. It was an
experience that I really can't describe other than to say I was floating.

Since that time it has helped me tremendously in many ways. For
example, when there is a lot of anxiety, tension, frustration, fear or
depression I will pray in tongues. I feel that it really helps me pull
out of those situations. By using the gift of tongues I feel it helps me
to become one in mind with Jesus and His will for me.

Priscilla

> I use tongues often to settle down before I pray or to help others to get closer to the Holy Spirit when I pray with them.

Wilbur

> I prayed in tongues right off! After they prayed for me following the baptism in the Spirit I prayed in tongues. I prayed all night long. I couldn't stop and I didn't want to stop. I felt light, elated; so happy. I pray in tongues mainly at night before I go to sleep peacefully. Also, when I'm feeling dry in conventional prayer I pray in tongues.

Rob

> After going to a *Life in the Spirit* week-end retreat, I remembered how so many of the others making the retreat began speaking in tongues, but I tried and nothing would come. Many times I was prayed over for the release of the gift of tongues, nothing happened. Finally, I went to a conference and attended a workshop on tongues where the teacher explained that we had control of the gift and the best way to begin was to praise the Lord in English. After praising the Lord in English, he said we were to keep making sounds of praise, but stop the English. When I tried as he directed, the gift of tongues was released and I was free to praise the Lord with sounds of my voice. Amen.

The gift of prayer is our direct communication with God, and just like any relationship, the more intimate the communication, the more profound the relationship. Tongues is one aspect of prayer that can catapult a person into deeper spiritual communication with the Triune God. If viewed as such, then more people can gain an authentic encounter with their first Love. Spiritual gifts, including the charism of tongues, forms the person to be more obedient to the movements of the Holy Spirit, thus building up the Church of Christ.

CONCLUSION

Just as the Father has sent his only Son, so Christ sent his apostles to all peoples. By the power of the Holy Spirit, Jesus bestowed many gifts upon the apostles to enable them to lay the foundation of the Church. He equips the Church today, just as he did the early Church, with an arsenal of spiritual gifts to enhance the spread of the gospel. The charism of tongues, being one of these spiritual weapons, has been exercised regularly from the very birth of the Church.

The resurrected Christ embodies the Church and, the Holy Spirit present as the Lord and Giver of life, vivifies its members. God desires his people to become divinized; to be filled with the Spirit of Christ. And it is the Spirit who forms Jesus within us. By His very essence He prompts us to love and to venture beyond ourselves; to edify others, especially within the Church community.

Prayer maintains and develops this response to the Holy Spirit. Among the forms of prayer that builds up the Church and the individual Christian, the charism of tongues must be included. The *prayer power* that tongues provides is open to all who desire it. This desire flows from the reception of the Holy Spirit, especially in Baptism, which is given through the Church.

Faith comes through hearing, hope comes through endurance, and love comes from doing. These virtues are only manifested through actions. The charism of tongues can be another vehicle of grace to strengthen these virtues, as it brings holiness for the individual and edification for the Church.

St. Paul, when instructing the Corinthians about spiritual gifts, insists that love be the motivation and the way of their desire to experience charismatic gifts. When these gifts operate on a level of unselfishness, they manifest a tremendous act of love by consoling with a word of wisdom or prophecy, by healing, or by praying in tongues for another.

The charism of tongues is a concrete manifestation of the Holy Spirit, either as personal prayer or for the ministry of edifying others. This gift (and sign) has love as its root and its fruit. Karl Stern in his book on psychiatry and religion, *The Third Revolution*, says there is only one way to determine if something is of God.

> "It is one very particular aspect of the 'nothing but.' If one scrutinizes the life history of any Saint or any mystic carefully enough, one always finds the psychological reason why the supernatural happened when it happened. When God comes into our life, He 'comes in handy.' To those who think exclusively in psychological terms, this makes the supernatural experience suspect. In the last analysis, there is only one perfectly reliable criterion. It is, by their fruits you shall know them."[196]

And the charism of tongues has proven to be an enduring and fruitful tree!

ADDENDUM:

Yielding to the Charism of Tongues

Receiving the charism of tongues as a gift of prayer is not as difficult as most people think. Frequently, our difficulty lies in yielding to the Holy Spirit. God gives the gift but fear, doubt, and lack of humility can inhibit us from yielding to the charism of tongues. Yielding is simply letting go; not resisting. The one who yields has trust, which reflects the amount of faith present, and where there is faith the Holy Spirit can work in freedom. Here are three simple steps that will help you yield to the gift of tongues.

1. Ask for the Gift

Jesus said, "Ask, and it will be given to you" (Mt. 7:7). If you desire the gift of tongues, including both praying in tongues and speaking in tongues with interpretation, you should not be afraid to pray and ask for it because God will not force these gifts on anyone. Even though some people have received tongues without directly petitioning God, the gift will probably not be received without asking. It is also well for us to understand that when Paul invites us to "earnestly desire the spiritual gifts" (1 Cor. 14:1), he wants to instill a sense of trust in actively seeking the charisms of the Holy Spirit.

2. Believe That the Holy Spirit Will Manifest the Gift

Sometimes we may not be afraid to ask for a particular

gift from God, but we can doubt that God can or will grant our request. God wants us to be full spiritually, and this includes different ways of praying. Jesus reminds us that if "we who are imperfect know how to give gifts, how much more will God give the Holy Spirit to those who ask Him." (Lk. 11:9). And if God is willing to give the very person of the Holy Spirit to us, He will also give the gifts, according to the movement of the Spirit.

3. Allow the Holy Spirit to Use Your Tongue and Voice

Plainly, you need to open your mouth and begin to speak. Many times humility is: "I can" rather than "I can't." How will praying or singing in tongues come forth if there is no sound coming from your voice or rolling off of your tongue? Yes, the Spirit gives the gift and guides the flow of tongues, but He wants you to receive the gift by participating freely and actively. By humbly giving the Holy Spirit permission to use your voice, you will begin to be free from fear and doubt. At this point, you are trusting in the movement of the Spirit.

Many people have received the gift of praying in tongues in a prayer group setting. The support of others helps us tremendously in yielding to the Spirit. Once the person feels comfortable in yielding to the Spirit, the prayer in tongues usually begins to flow out. Therefore, the tongues of the group can be the catalyst for a beginner to "kick-start" his or her new gift of praise. This often happens when the sound of the tongues is imitated by the beginner. Many times the starting point comes from repeating certain words or phrases like

"Alleluia" or "Praise you, Jesus" or "Come Holy Spirit". This opens the mouth with words of praise to God and the person can easily change from the vernacular to praying or singing in tongues; uttering "mysteries in the Spirit" (1 Cor. 14:2).

Mimicking the sound of the tongues of others in the group may seem awkward at first, but soon a shift will take place. The person will notice the movement from just making sound to the power of praising God in the Spirit.

And yet apart from the support of a group, some have come into the gift of tongues in a variety of ways: some by individually stepping out in faith by praising God in their native language and the tongues came from their prayer; some by listening to others singing in tongues on a video or audio tape; others have used their imagination and visualized themselves praying in tongues and the charism eventually came forth; and still others, because of their openness, received the gift suddenly in a surprising moment, similar to the accounts in the Acts of the Apostles (Acts 2:1-4; 10:44-46; 19:1-6).

Once the person seeking the charism of tongues yields in humility, fear and doubt diminish; then it is just a matter of time before the prayer in tongues will develop. This gift of prayer is simple, so for those who desire and seek it earnestly, the Holy Spirit will pour out the charism. If it was St. Paul's desire for all the Corinthians to have the gift of tongues, does it not make sense that the Holy Spirit would have an even greater desire to bestow this gift on us?

END NOTES PART III

[153] Hampsch, *The Gift of Tongues*, Tape #2.

[154] Ibid.

[155] Ibid.

[156] Ibid.

[157] Ibid.

[158] Ibid.

[159] Ensely, *Sounds of Wonder*, p. 17.

[160] Ibid., p. 74.

[161] Ibid., p. 75.

[162] Hampsch, *The Gift of Tongues,* Tape #2.

[163] Ibid.

[164] Ibid.

[165] Ibid.

[166] Ranaghan, *Catholic Pentecostals Today*, p. 144.

[167] Hampsch, *The Gift of Tongues,* Tape #2.

[168] Kilian McDonnell, O.S.B., *Christian Initiation and Baptism in the Spirit,* p. 323.

[169] Hampsch, *The Gift of Tongues,* Tape #2.

[170] DeGrandis, *Gifts of the Spirit,* "Maturing in Tongues and Interpretation," Tape #5.

[171] Hampsch, *The Gift of Tongues,* Tape #2.

[172] DeGrandis, *Gifts of the Spirit,* Tape #5.

[173] I have personally witnessed both Maria and Fr. Zimmer exercise these gifts. I was told that Maria prayed for the gift to speak Italian because of the many pilgrims from Italy who came to Medjugorje. Fr. Zimmer has also told me that the gift of other languages is beneficial when he is hearing confessions.

[174] DeGrandis, *Gifts of the Spirit,* Tape #5.

[175] Hampsch, *The Gift of Tongues,* Tape #2.

[176] Sullivan, *Charisms and the Charismatic Renewal,* p. 144.

[177] Cornwell, *The Gift of Tongues Today,* pp. 24-25.

[178] DeGrandis, *The Gift of Tongues*, p. 9.

[179] Hampsch, *The Gift of Tongues,* Tape #2.

[180] Ibid.

[181] Ibid.

[182] Vincent Walsh, *The Key to the Charismatic Renewal in the Catholic Church,* p. 56.

[183] Robert Faricy, , S.J., "Contemplation: Gift of the Spirit," *Renewal in the Spirit, Newsletter for the Renewal of the Charisms of Religious Life:* Summer 1982.

[184] Ibid.

[185] *Theological and Pastoral Orientations on the Catholic Charismatic Renewal,* p. 52.

[186] DeGrandis, *Gifts of the Spirit*, Tape #5.

[187] Ibid.

[188] Suenens, *A New Pentecost?*, p. 103.

[189] DeGrandis, *Gifts of the Spirit*, Tape #5.

[190] Ranaghan, *Catholic Pentecostals Today*, p. 42.

[191] DeGrandis, *Gifts of the Spirit*, "Deliverance," Tape #12.

[192] Ibid., Tape #5 and #12.

[193] Ibid., Tape #1.

[194] Suenens, *A New Pentecost?*, p. 103.

[195] DeGrandis, *Gifts of the Spirit*, Tape #5.

[196] Ranaghan, *Catholic Pentecostals Today*, p. 151.

BIBLIOGRAPHY

Aquinas. *Summa Theologiae,* Vol. 45. Roland Potter, O.P., ed. Black Friars, Manchester, England, 1970.

Augustine. "The Retractions", Vol. 60. *The Fathers of the Church.* Edited by Sr. Mary Inez Bogen, R.S.M., Ph.D. Washington, DC: Catholic University Press, 1968.

Barret, C.K. "Chapter 14 - Spiritual Gifts," *The New International Commentary on the New Testament: The First Epistle to the Corinthians.* New York & Evanston: Harper and Row, 1968.

Clark, Edward. "The Communal Charism of Education And Its Application To Catholic High Schools In The United States", (Ph.D. Dissertatio ad Doctoratum in Facultate Theologiae Pontificiae Universitatis Gregorianae, Roma). 1988.

Cornwell, Malcom, C.P. *The Gift of Tongues Today.* Pecos, NM: Dove Publications, 1975.

DeGrandis, Robert, S.S.J. *The Gift of Tongues.* New Orleans : Robert DeGrandis, publisher, 1983.

————. *Gifts of the Spirit: A Complete Teaching.* Albuquerque, NM: Hand Productions, 1986. Audiocassette.

————. *The Gift of Miracles.* Ann Arbor, MI: Servant Books, 1991.

Dunn, James, D.G. *Baptism in the Holy Spirit.* Naperville, IL: Alec R. Allenson Inc., 1970.

Ensely, Eddie. *Sounds of Wonder.* New York: Paulist Press, 1977.

Faricy, Robert, S.J. "Contemplation: Gift of the Spirit," *Renewal in the Spirit,* Newsletter for the Renewal of the Charisms of Religious Life. Rome, Italy, Summer 1982.

Flannery, Austin, O.P., ed. *The Documents of the Second Vatican Council.* "St. Paul Editions," Boston: Daughters of St.Paul, 1988.

Hahn, Scott. *The New Pentecost,* "What is the Cost of Pentecost?", Tape #2. West Covina, CA: St. Joseph Communications, Inc., 1992. Audiocassette.

Hampsch, John, C.M.F. *The Gift of Tongues.* Los Angeles: Claretian Tape Ministry. Audiocassette.

Hardon, John. *The Catholic Catechism.*

Johanson, B.C. "Tongues, A Sign For Unbelievers?: A Structural and Exegetical study of I Corinthians XIV. 20-25," *New Testament Studies,* 25 (1979), 180-203.

John Paul II. *Christifideles Laici.* Boston: Daughters of St. Paul, 1988.

———. "The Beginning of the Church's Mission," General Audience September 20, 1989, *The Pope Speaks,* 35:1, (1990), 38.

Kelsey, Morton. *Tongue Speaking: The History and Meaning Of Charismatic Experience.* Rev. ed. New York: Crossword Pub. Co., 1981.

Kiesling, Christopher, O.P. *Confirmation and the Full Life of the Spirit.* Cincinnati: St. Anthony Messenger Press, 1973.

Laurentin, René. *Catholic Pentecostalism.* Translated by Matthew J. O'Connell. Garden City, NY: Image Books, 1978.

Lederle, H.I. *Treasures Old and New: Interpretation of "Spirit-Baptism" in the Charismatic Renewal Movement.* Peabody, MA: Hendrickson Pub., 1988.

Martinez, Luis, D.D. *The Sanctifier.* Translated from the Spanish by Sr. M. Aquinas, O.S.U. Paterson, NJ: St. Anthony Guild, 1957. Reprinted by The Daughters of St. Paul, 1982.

May, Herbert and Metzger, Bruce, eds. *The New Oxford Annotated Bible-Revised Standard Edition.* New York: Oxford University Press, Inc., 1977.

McDonnell, Kilian, O.S.B. and Montague, George, S.M. *Christian Initiation and Baptism in the Holy Spirit: Evidence from the First Eight Centuries.* Collegeville, MN: Michael Glazier Books, Liturgical Press, 1991.

Mills, Watson E. *Glossolalia: A Bibliography, Studies in the Bible and Early Christianity.* Vol. 6. New York and Toronto: Edwin Mellen Press, 1985.

Murphy-O'Connor, Jerome. "The First Letter to the Corinthians." *The New Jerome Biblical Commentary.* NJ: Prentice Hall, (1990), 811-12.

O'Collins, Gerald, S.J. and Farrugio, Edward, S.J. *A Concise Dictionary of Theology.* New York: Paulist Press, 1991.

Paul VI. Address to the General Audience of November 29,1972. *L' Osservatore Romano,* 7 December 1972, English language edition.

———. "The Holy Spirit and the Life of the Church," Address to the General Audience, Oct. 12, 1966, *The Pope Speaks* 12:1, (1967), 79-81.

Ranaghan, Kevin and Dorothy. *Catholic Pentecostals Today.* Rev. ed. Southbend, IN: Charismatic Renewal Services Inc., 1983.

Richardson, William. "Liturgical Order and Glossolalia in I Corinthian 14.26c-33a." *New Testament Studies* 32 (1986): 144-153.

Roebeck, Cecil M., Jr., ed. *Charismatic Experiences in History.* Peabody, MA: Hendrickson Publishers, 1985.

Samarin, William J. *Tongues of Men and Angels.* New York: MacMillan Co., 1972.

Staton, Knofel. *Spiritual Gifts For Christians Today.* Joplin, MO: College Press, 1973.

Stoddard, Charles Warren. *Saint Anthony, The Wonder-Worker of Padua.* 1896. Reprint, Rockford, IL: TAN Books and Publishers Inc., 1971.

Suenens, Leon Joseph Cardinal. *A New Pentecost?* New York: Seabury Press, 1975.

Sullivan, Francis, S.J. *Charisms and Charismatic Renewal.* Ann Arbor, MI: Servant Books, 1982.

"Theological and Pastoral Orientations on the Catholic Charismatic Renewal." *Word of Life* (Notre Dame, IN): 1974. First published in Malines, Belgium, May, 1974.

The Rites of the Catholic Church, Vol.1. "Christian Initiation of Adults." New York: Pueblo Publishing Co., 1985.

Tugwell, Simon, O.P. *Did You Receive the Spirit?* Springfield, IL: Template Publishing, 1972.

————. "So Who's a Pentecostal Now?" *New Black Friars,* no. 57 (1976). 418.

Walsh, Vincent M. *A Key to Charismatic Renewal in the Catholic Church.* St. Meinrad, IN: Abbey Press, 1976.

.

Order Form

Postal Orders: Mission West Communications
P. O. Box 2369, Santa Maria, CA 93457-2369. USA.

The Charism of Tongues: A Gift of Prayer and Edification

Please send_____book(s) @ $7.95 to:**(Please Print)**

Name: _____

Add: _____

City: _____

State: _____Zip: _____

Phone No. _____

Signature: _____

Sales Tax:
Please add sales tax for books shipped to California addresses.

Shipping (No COD'S)
Book Rate: $2.25 for first book and 75 cents for each additional book.
(Surface shipping may take three to four weeks.)

Priority Shipping: $3.00 per book.

Amount enclosed: _____

Information: Call 805-937-2766   **Fax: 805-937-9114**
CT1196MS